DOG TALES

an unleashed collection of true stories

EDITED BY

Andrea Cleghorn, Elizabeth Banks, Nancy Brigham,
Len Charney, and Kevin Fahey

All the essays in this collection are nonfiction. In certain cases, names have been changed to preserve confidentiality and anonymity. There are no composites. All events have been reported to the best of each author's knowledge.

Published by Ginkgo Books, Bedford, Massachusetts 01730

ISBN: 978-0-9969354-3-2

A collection of essays written by 33 different authors, edited by Cleghorn, Andrea; Banks, Elizabeth; Brigham, Nancy; Charney, Len, and Fahey, Kevin

Designer: Nancy Daugherty

Dog Tales: An Unleashed Collection of True Stories
p. cm.
Books Trade paperback ISBN: 978-09969354-3-2

Cover photo by Len Charney

Ginkgo Books
87 South Road, Bedford, MA 01730

PRINTED IN THE UNITED STATES OF AMERICA

Dedicated to dogs everywhere,
who depend on us
to provide safe, joyful lives
in return for the love
they so freely give to us.

All proceeds from the sale of this book
go to Caring Canines,
a visiting therapy dog organization.

The Tales

A Dog's View

– Donal Fitzgerald –

They tell people I am a Miniature Schnauzer, bred after the First World War in Germany with the object of reducing the rat population. That's too much history for a girl like me to dwell on.

My story is much more recent. I was born on the east coast of England in the scenic and quintessentially English town of Southwold in the county of Suffolk in the year 2007, New Year's Day, to be precise. My owners adopted me when I was 3 months old, together with my brother. Murchy and I joined a happy household where I quickly found a niche for myself. There was another older dog, blind and half daft, called Henry. He was a Cavalier King Charles Spaniel, but a poor specimen of one, if memory serves me. I accepted him, but if truth be known, I ignored him, for he was neither chivalrous nor playful, and when he grinned, he was all gums.

Being someone who believed you had to do what you had to do to survive, I got on with life and made the most of what the dice had dealt me. I loved the North Sea beaches, the country trails, and the people's generosity of spirit to all things four-legged. They told me the skies over Suffolk were the biggest in the world, and to me, they were not just big; they were heaven unveiled. The light, which inspired the artist Constable, among others, lifted my soul, and the other dogs were a joy to meet, each with his own story, which I would try to listen to when my parents had the good manners to allow me to stop and chat.

We lived a charmed life, and looking back on it now, I know I was lucky compared to some.

I remember talking with Bruno from Peppermint Farm, where we went on Saturday mornings to purchase our garden produce, and boy, did he have a story to tell – hard work, poor digs, long hours, and a hard-of-heart master.

I, in comparison, was known on our Crescent as the "princess," a term seldom used to my face, but I secretly enjoyed it anyway. My brother had a heart of gold and a wholesome laugh, compensated for old gummy. Alas, that heart was not to beat forever, which reminds me, we also had some dark days.

Well, listening to this sepia-toned story, you might ask what went wrong, and it is a question well worth asking.

Sometime around the London Olympics, I cannot help but remember, it as it played havoc with my daily walks. My parents spoke about moving house, and I can't pretend I wasn't excited. New frontiers and new challenges keep a girl young. I heard them mention Ireland, which sounded delicious, probably a place with beaches better than we had at home. I didn't discourage the idea but decided I would tread carefully, for I knew them, although kind, to be both given to moments of foolishness and impulsivity.

Four years later, here I am in the southwest corner of Ireland, and I fear that their foolishness is my misfortune. I have accumulated the rewards of age and thrown away the benefits of experience. Shortly after getting to this place, they took me to the vet for a checkup.

"Oh," said he, shaking his head. "Cataracts. There isn't a lot to be done."

Oh, no, I thought, oh no. I bet there isn't, but if I were human and had a voice, I would be treated to the best that money could buy in the ophthalmology suite. A dog's life has its limitations.

For good measure, the vet removed all of my rotting teeth. I can't quite see that they could get me dentures, as it does sound a bit excessive. I now think more sympathetically of old gummy Henry, whom they buried in the garden on the Suffolk coast.

Peppermint Farm, I hear you say, by way of cold comfort. Yes, there is a farm here as well, and a farmer who stops his tractor to talk with my parents sometimes. I heard the uncouth old wretch ask my father once, "Would ye not be better getting rid of her? She is well past her prime"

I could respond with a comment that would shine a light on his ample shortcomings, but I desisted, for a lady needs to wear her dignity like a nice cut dress, with a style and flair that catches the eye. That's the way I was brought up, and I won't change now.

Oh yes, I almost forgot the big skies of Suffolk. Yes, lots of them here, in Kerry, too, but I never get to see them for the clouds, the incessant rain, and the infernal wind. I sit here in my basket as I recount this story, and the drumming on the roof is like the mocking laughter of the gods. These parents of mine have made their decision, and they seem happy with it; maybe it's their turn to be rewarded. I am pleased for them.

As for me, maybe it is the getting old I do not agree with – my gummy smile, ripening cataracts, and painful joints – all reminders of my accumulating years. When I look back on my life and consider the love surrounding me, I know my blessings have been as numerous as the sands on the beach. Maybe, like that nice cut dress, age is to be worn with dignity and a smile, a badge of having survived tougher times, and that is just what this girl intends to go on doing.

I bid you, dear reader, a very good night. I am returning to my basket and will think of that drumming on the roof as gentle background music to my pleasant dreams.

Our Mountain Girl Awaits

– Susan Ellis –

She was a beauty – sleek and elegant, petite but powerful. She could run all day if you let her, but she was patient enough to lie and wait for her daily walk while I was busy making lunches and getting the children off to school. German Shorthair Pointers were bred as hunting dogs and great home companions. Laney really fit the bill.

Most days, we were limited to a three-mile walk. There wasn't time to do much more. We loved to hike as a family, which meant that on weekends, we would take her out to the woods and let her off-leash. We'd walk the marked paths, and she would stay with us for the most part, but occasionally, she'd take off, blasting through the trees like a hawk set on prey. I imagined she was happiest at those times when she was able to experience the pure joy of running circles around us. We would lose sight of her, and then the sound of her running would fade, but 10 minutes later, she'd be back by our side, walking along as one of the pack.

I suppose I developed a sense of security that, no matter what, she would be back to check in with us before much time had passed. That worked well for us until, on one hike, we made a stupid choice.

The weather that day started fine but clouded up as we walked. When we reached the beginning of the sheer granite that makes up the top of that mountain in New Hampshire, it was clear a storm was coming. Typically, that means it's time to turn around, but we were close to the summit and hadn't done this particular walk in a long time.

Laney was off running in the woods. We couldn't wait for her. Still, we decided to go for it, hit the summit, and turn around at once to make our way down. As we walked, I kept calling for my dog, but she was nowhere near. The sky was increasingly ominous, and as an experienced hiker, I wondered what I had been thinking when I agreed to keep going.

We got to the top and back to the trees before the storm started. I assumed Laney had lost our scent when we started walking on the rocky mountaintop. She may have gone farther than usual, confident like us that she knew what she was doing and would be OK. I called and called, but Laney did not return. We moved fast coming back, but it took about an hour and a half to get to the bottom.

Finally, we reached the trailhead. We felt stressed, depressed, and guilty. My mind was racing as we discussed what we might do about our missing dog. And then I saw something I never expected. Laney was there, sitting at the very end of the path. She looked like a child, fidgeting and looking around but not moving from the spot where she was fixed. She caught my eye and ran to us, doing her happy dance. A young couple who were watching her asked, "Is this your dog?

"She wouldn't move," they said. "She refused to come with us. She sat there for the past half hour watching, like she knew you would come to get her."

My immediate feeling was relief. I knew we were lucky that we had not suffered serious injury and that we were able to leave intact as a family. Since then, however, I've thought about the day many times and felt chilled by the thought of all the things that could have gone wrong. It has remained for me the most potent reminder of why when something seems like a bad idea, you should probably not do it.

Note I said probably.

Yes, it was a bad idea to go for the summit, mainly because I had no idea where Laney was, or whether she or one of us would get hit by lightning. As our family walked to an exposed spot at the top of a mountain, I thought Laney would follow us. Despite the facts though, I can't help remembering how happy Laney was to run freely through the woods that day or how delighted we were to see her there waiting for us, reminding us how important we were to her and she to us.

This does not mean I intended or do intend to continue making stupid choices for the rest of my life. I learned my lesson that day. As a memory, though, this one stands out as one of the best, making it hard to feel bad about the original choice. Dogs so often remind us of their unwavering devotion. That devotion is reinforced by responsible pet ownership that prevents them from getting into trouble like getting lost far from home or a lightning disaster. The idea that she covered for us that day by doing the right thing when we did not stuns me every time I consider her remarkable performance. She was smart. I knew that about her. I doubt she thought it through as I should have, but she did make the right choice in heading down without us and waiting until we came out. We made more mistakes in life, I'm sure, but few as big as this and none with results that ended so well.

A Loving Tribute to Rascal

– Joseph Lafo –

Some years ago, I was working on a project at the University of New Hampshire and drove there once a week for two years. Occasionally, for a change on the drive home from the always-crowded freeway, I would take the back roads, a calming respite from the aggressions of several lanes of commuters, a large percentage of whom were angry. On one such backroad diversion, I passed a sign in front of a house: "Black Labrador Retriever Puppies." The thought of having a dog – you know, "for our two sons" – began its gestation period. It was a short gestation period.

Remembering the look on the boys' faces when we surprised them by bringing Fuzzy the Cat home in a loosely wrapped box, from which a beautiful orange and white kitten jumped out, was beyond compare; I decided that another surprise was in order. Soon after that, I went back to that country road and found the house with the sign. I drove down a long driveway to the house, which had several adjacent kennels – they raised registered Labs. Once in the house, I was introduced to Rascal's parents, who were both calm and friendly around the stranger, as Labs are inclined to be.

Then, they brought in three puppies from a recent litter. The puppy, who would be named Rascal, was charming and very calm – more so than his siblings – and a few minutes later, he was in a holding cage in the back of the car, heading for his new home.

When I arrived home, the boys, as expected, were pretty excited. Fuzzy, on the other hand – by then, 8 years old or so – was not impressed and distanced himself from this large intruder. For Rascal's 13 years of life, despite not a single act of aggression by Rascal toward our three cats, Fuzzy diligently kept that separation, even when Rascal's nose sniffed within an inch of Fuzzy's tail.

My wife, Rachel, it must be said, was as unimpressed as Fuzzy, maybe more so, which, years later, she still reminds me of occasionally. "How could you get a dog without even asking me?" she wonders aloud. "It's something both adults in a couple would discuss prior to getting one!" Fortunately, Rascal's considerable charm and quiet nature won everyone over, including Rachel.

A couple of weeks after Rascal's arrival, I was on a business trip and called home. Rachel was standing in the kitchen, and we chit-chatted about this and that, and then, "I'm still mad about you not telling me about Rascal."

Followed by, "Oh, here comes Rascal now. He is a sweet dog and... What! No! No! He's pooping on the kitchen floor!"

"I have to go," I said.

Fortunately, Rascal took to training and, in a class with a dozen or so other dogs of all types, handily took home the coveted Prize Bone as Best in Class. I worked with Rascal every evening, including taking him to the town high school football field. He would sit on the zero-yard line, while I first walked to the 5-yard line and said come; sometimes he would. But he got much better; by the end of the training classes, Rascal would sit right there as I walked to the opposite end of the field, 100 yards away, without looking back. Calling him, he would immediately start running, full speed, for the length of the field and sit in front of me.

✡

What causes one, donning a winter coat, scarf, long johns, gloves, boots, and woolen cap, to eschew the warmth of a well-built fire and hot drink to trudge into the quiet of a late winter's night during a snowstorm, the opening of the screen door pushing away the accumulating new snow on the porch, to make way for a cold departure?

Partially, I suppose, because few others are so engaged as I walk past house after house in quiet repose, thereby left to my own thoughts with only the creak of leafless branches, sounding as clear as a woodpecker's drumbeat in an early morning forest falling to my ears, with little worry of the interference of a snowblower's wail. No, I could walk unhindered, with only an occasional sweep of a car's headlights passing fleetingly over me, the car tires crunching on the icy snow of the road.

For many years, of course, Rascal was always ready for such a walk no matter the hour or season; he especially loved plowing through the deep snow even as I took the somewhat easier path of the cleared sidewalk. Together, we went our separate ways: me contemplating the cold and the stars above, while Rascal, led, as always, by his nose, pursued whatever he found appealing under the snow. He looked up occasionally, noting my whereabouts, breaching the white, crystalline waves like a whale in the ocean, taking a breath, and diving again. For every foot I walked, Rascal walked three or more.

On midnight walks, we often made our way to the Old Burying Ground, a local, historic cemetery that was laid out at the time of the town's beginning in 1729. Under the light of the moon, Rascal and I played hide and seek among the slate headstones, several of which marked veterans of the Revolutionary War.

On winter nights, joined by Rascal, I gathered wood for a fire, trudging through the snow to the wood pile, chopping logs into appropriate sizes, and lugging them into the house, where I would find three cats lined up in front of the fireplace, in anticipation of the coming warmth. I got the kindling going, piled on the logs, and sat back, giving the front-row seat to Rascal and the cats, each asleep in a matter of a few minutes.

Rascal met skunks on several occasions, and the exchange was always in favor of the skunk. Why, we wondered, didn't he learn from those painful experiences? In the aftermath of a bath of some unpleasant concoction recommended to alleviate the overpowering smell, why didn't he forgo chasing any animal with a white stripe down its back? At night, Rascal would be out for just a few minutes, and suddenly, the whole house would be filled with the overpowering odor of a-skunk-just-outside-our-windows.

While Rascal tolerated our cats and absolutely loved one of them, when it came to any other cat, he was *Canis lupus familiaris*. He always gave chase, though not for long – he knew they were unobtainable. Rascal had an equal enthusiasm for squirrels and occasionally crows; he enjoyed stirring them up even if they were beyond his grasp.

One day, we got a call from the bank that was at the end of our street, on the corner of the main road through town.

"Do you have a dog named Rascal?" they asked.

"Yes," I replied, "Why do you ask?"

"Well, he came into the bank when the door opened for a customer and laid down. He likes watching the bank do its business." With Rascal's leash in hand, I took a walk.

After Rascal, we moved from the Boston area to Vancouver, B.C., and we missed his presence and kind soul; he didn't have a mean bone in his body, and he barked just a handful of times in his life.

One of the more noticeable aspects of Vancouverites was their love of dogs. They were everywhere and out in force on the city. I frequently stopped for a wagged tail, a pat on the head, a stroke of the back, and a few minutes' chat with the owner with their dog at their side or, as was occasionally the case, hanging from a shoulder bag, checking out the world from a higher perspective.

No matter the breed, they all reminded me of Rascal, who was, simply put, one of The Greatest Dogs Ever. In this, of course, I know I sound like every other dog owner, and you can see it on the face of, and hear it in conversation with many of them.

In science, it is generally believed that all of today's astonishing variety of dogs have a common, original ancestor, a long-extinct species of wolf. Over many millennia of domestication, dogs have been bred and trained to perform many tasks. Most importantly, dogs have another admirable attribute: they provide their owners with an empathetic ear and paw, as Rascal certainly did.

We Named Her Brigid for the Saint

— Nancy Brigham —

We called ourselves the St. Brigid's mafia, the 25 or 30 families who became involved in the socially progressive time of Vatican II; we refused to give up even when our new pastor wanted no part of us or our ideas. When Father John Crowley was assigned to our church, his leadership and encouragement helped us form an activist community. Then, the diocese suddenly transferred him to an impoverished parish in the inner city and stationed him in a drafty old rectory that contained 11 bedrooms, 10 of them empty.

When he called, John's voice echoed over the phone in the empty rooms of his house. Not one to complain, he did admit he was having trouble making friends with the people in his new parish. "When I take a walk," he said, "I have a hard time getting a hello out of anybody."

Over glasses of wine one night, my friend Barbara and I decided that John needed a dog to keep him company and brighten up his life. The next day, we went to the local shelter and stood outside for a few minutes, trying to decide exactly what we were looking for. Was it a puppy, an older dog, a small dog, a large dog, a lap dog, a watchdog?

Then a woman pulled up next to us and opened the trunk of her car wherein were five puppies, five beautiful raucous gray and black puppies. Well, four raucous ones and one that huddled in the back shivering. We both knew that had to be John's dog. We named her Brigid for the saint and took her home with us.

The next afternoon, with Brigid bathed and fed, we drove downtown trying to devise a stratagem to convince John he wanted a puppy. To sweeten the deal, we brought food, bowls, and puppy pads. As soon as he realized what we intended, John began to shake his head negatively, and as we persisted, he put his hands out as if to ward us off. Peeking out of Barbara's jacket, Brigid was fascinated by his moving hands and tentatively swiped at them. The cuter she got, the more vehemently John made his excellent arguments for why he could not have a puppy.

Then, like a *deus ex machina*, the phone rang. The phone sat in the hall outside the kitchen, and when John went to answer it, he closed the door for privacy. That might have been what gave us the idea. Telling Brigid that it would be OK, we put water in one bowl and puppy food in the other. With hugs, kisses, and apologies, we left her pitiful and scared cowering in the corner of the cavernous kitchen and took off. We looked behind us several times on the drive home to make sure John wasn't following us.

Of course, I wasn't there when John returned to the kitchen and looked around, finding us gone and Brigid still there. She must have been a pitiful sight. She needed comfort, love, and gentleness, all the things John Crowley could provide better than any other priest I ever met.

Barbara and I kept low profiles for two weeks, and then we called. "How is Brigid?" we asked, fingers crossed. John started to laugh and said, "Thank you both. I don't think I realized how lonely I was until Brigid arrived. She has taken control of me and the parish. Now, when I walk, everyone says hello, and people come to see her when I bring her to church. Attendance at mass has increased every Sunday."

"You bring her to church?"

"She insists. She likes to sleep at the feet of the statue of Mary. And, when I hear confessions, she sits outside the box and herds people inside. I know she puts them in a better frame of mind."

"You mean they don't feel like sinners anymore?"

"Oh, they know they're sinners, but Brigid is full of forgiveness."

The man was besotted. Everywhere that John went, the dog went. It was JohnandBrigid, one word. I would hear tales from friends about John's visits, which were apparently highlighted by Brigid's success in monopolizing the best seat in the house. My friend Tony said in mock outrage, that Brigid nudged him off his own sofa so she could stretch out and nap. "And John just smiled," he added.

I only saw John and Brigid together once, a chance meeting in Lexington Center. Even from a distance, I could tell that Brigid had grown into a beautiful mid-size dog who carried herself with the unconscious confidence of a much-loved pet. She stuck close to John's side and, although she seemed relaxed, I could see from the way she scrutinized her surroundings that if anyone threatened her master, she would spring to his defense. In all the years he stayed in the inner city, John was never harassed; I'm pretty sure I know why.

My Heart and the Quiet Ones

– Jenny Stewart –

We stopped by the shelter on a Saturday morning just at the first stages of discussion about getting a family dog; there were no pet supplies at home, and no intention to take one home with us that day. As we were getting ready to leave, I had a love-at-first-sight moment when a nervous black dog passed us in the lobby on her way to the shelter after a week at a foster home. Twenty minutes later, the pup (shelter name Daria, soon renamed Rosie by us) was family, sitting in the backseat of the minivan with my three small children.

We were told the dog was 1 or 2 years old, likely already had a litter of puppies, had been transported from a kill shelter in the South, and was a Lab mix, but it's clear, and later confirmed with DNA testing, that Rosie was mainly a gentle little Pit. She was timid, filthy, wracked with nervous shakes, and carsick almost immediately.

The first couple of weeks of transitioning to our home were not pretty. In addition to the expected rescue dog warming-up period and Rosie's innate personality of anxiety and wariness, our new dog didn't feel great. She had a lot of weight to gain and had fluids draining from her eyes, ears, and other locations. She was recovering from spay surgery, on a dewormer and antibiotics, and was itchy all over. She was throwing up and bleeding from places one might not expect.

She was scared of many things, but she was very comfortable spending her days recovering in the dog bed we got for her. So we let her. We'd pet her and whisper gentle healing words to her, let her sleep, and deliver snacks right to her mouth so she didn't even have to lift her head. But we also had those 8-, 6-, and 4-year-olds who just adopted their first family dog.

So Rosie was sometimes dragged to the school bus stop. Or greeted with squeals when the kids' friends came for a playdate. Or had toys tossed in her vicinity, waggled in her line of sight, and pressed toward her snout in an attempt to engage her. And a dozen times per day, Rosie, at nearly 30 pounds, was picked up awkwardly by our wispy 8-year-old.

Mary would silently and undramatically scoop up the poor dog when she thought they were alone. The two would hold still for a couple of minutes, like a cherub-faced porcelain Hummel figurine and her little lamb, and then Mary would gently put Rosie back to whatever the dog was originally doing. Mary would quietly move about her day and return to repeat the ritual at a regular pace.

"Mary put the dog down. Let her rest," I'd say while making dinner and seeing Mary out of the corner of my eye, standing perfectly still with the dog in her arms. But 45 minutes later, the dog, looking at me with resignation, would again be in Mary's arms. "Just give Rosie a hug with her feet on the ground." And Mary, gently placing Rosie back into her bed and arranging blankets around her would insist, "I'm practicing." "For what?" "In case we need it."

Rosie slowly started to heal, recover, and acclimate to our home. She remained silent, sweet, and gentle, but began to get more energy. She learned her name. She stopped bleeding, oozing, and itching and started gaining weight. Rosie loved to go to the school bus stop in the morning, and after dinner, she liked to play with the toys we offered.

She learned some new tricks. Her tail wagged nonstop, and she made some dog friends in the neighborhood.

And after about a month in the house, while cleaning up pancakes from breakfast, we discovered that Rosie was missing. We searched the house. We looked in the backyard. We were getting on our shoes and grabbing car keys to frantically search the neighborhood when calmly and quietly, coming up the front walk, was bed-headed barefoot Mary. Wearing only a nightie and a satisfied smile on her face, still sticky from breakfast, Mary was carrying Rosie like a lamb.

"I knew I was practicing for a reason," she said.

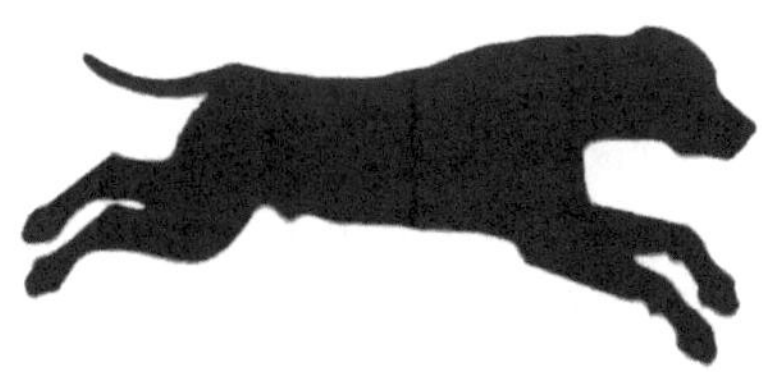

Midnight Rescue

– John Claflin –

My childhood neighborhood was largely unsupervised, feral kids with mostly good intentions. I was one of a core of five kids, but on this 30-degree winter's day, we were six, as Chris Russell tagged along. None of us minded; we all liked Chris, but he could be intense. So, Kevin, Wayne, Mickey, Louis, Chris, Chris' dog Midnight, and I headed out of the neighborhood in search of an adventure. Wayne was the oldest by one year. The rest of us were 11.

We decided we'd visit the train trestle, which was our primary source of fun during the summer. The frame separated two small bodies of water, giving us access to both sides for jumping in. The drop from the edge to the water wasn't more than five feet, but it felt like 20 to us. The purpose of our journey this time was to see what the trestle looked like during the winter.

Midnight was a plump Black Lab, friendly to the point of absurdity, the kind of dog that would lick the hand of a home invader. He was a legend in the neighborhood as he apparently believed none of our houses were off-limits. Given the chance, he would wander right in the front door and be the family's dog for a while, then head back out. There was no leash law in our town in 1974, and Midnight kept his journeys to our five houses exclusively. He was a joy.

So Midnight became the seventh member of our group, and we headed toward the trestle. The distance was more than a mile, and I remember thinking that the pads on Midnight's paws might get irritated by the pavement. Midnight strolled alongside us without any problems.

The six of us humans had completely different personalities. Wayne was a hard worker who started mowing lawns before any of us understood what money was. By the age of 12, Wayne had several hundred dollars in the bank, which seemed excessive to us. Kevin was the mechanical engineer of the group. He could fix anything that we'd broken before our parents got home. Louis was the comic book nerd with an odd passion for marching bands. Mickey was our explosives guy. He could procure gunpowder and fireworks in minutes. Chris was our part-time technology guy. Chris had his own home office filled with electronics and his most prized possession, a full CB set up with a standalone power mic. I always felt that Chris didn't think us to be as cerebral as his other friends, but our adventures were superior. This journey was no different.

On our way, we all speculated as to what we would see. We all agreed that the trestle would not look anything like its summer appearance. At two-thirds of the way, we had to leave the paved road and make our way down to the railroad tracks through a wooded area. It hadn't occurred to us that the snow might be a problem, but arriving at this wooded passage, we discovered that the sheet of ice on top of the snow was thick enough to support our weight – obstacle overcome.

Once we reached the railroad tracks, we were in breaking-the-law territory. In 1974, Massachusetts had a unique arm of the police called the MDC (Metropolitan District Commission). Their job was to patrol the reservoirs and state lands. They had the authority to arrest or detain individuals, so we were always on the lookout for the olive-green Plymouth Dusters they all drove.

The bitter cold wind coming off the reservoir had blown the snow off the crushed stone mounds under the tracks. Again, my mind went to Midnight's paws and I asked Chris, our most cerebral friend, if this was something Midnight could handle. He assured me that Midnight was fine. It was a short walk along the tracks until we reached our destination. At first, it seemed underwhelming, but a closer look uncovered how the moving water caused holes to open in the ice around the mouth of the trestle. Daring each other to walk out onto the ice ensued. Mickey, being the explosives and risk-taking guy, tossed a heavy stick about 10 feet out on the ice to check its strength.

Bounding from behind us, Midnight came forward in full sprint... he had his eye on that stick. We all made failed attempts to catch his collar, but it was over in seconds. He leaped from the trestle's edge and directly into the open water. Instant panic was written on his face. Desperately trying to lift his paws high enough to reach the ice's edge, Midnight began to yelp. Without thinking, I dived in. As I hit the water, I remembered that bulky clothing like jackets, boots, or even regular shoes could cause a person to drown. I'd seen this depicted on a hunting show on TV, but it was too late. Everything had to stay on.

Midnight was about 10 feet away. The cold hadn't hit me yet. I swam as best I could and grabbed Midnight's collar, instantly adding his weight to mine. At this point, I thought we were both gone. I just kept tugging and pulling, seeing stars at one point. I turned my body toward shore and somehow managed to flop and kick my way there. Midnight was the first out; I was a distant second. My clothes must have weighed an additional 40 pounds, but I awkwardly grabbed at the rocks below me and shimmied myself out of the water and onto the jagged shore next to the trestle. By this time, everyone was down at the water's edge, scrambling to pull me up. It took several of them to get me entirely on land.

Midnight seemingly had no issues from his near-drowning experience and walked home with us, acting as if nothing had happened.

I think one of the gang sacrificed his jacket to me for the trek back home. Mickey felt terrible about tossing the stick out onto the ice. Chris felt terrible for letting Midnight tag along with us. But the exhilaration of Midnight's rescue and a second chance at life overcame all of us as we walked home.

What's For Dinner?

– Brenda Fraser –

The baby was finally asleep. I was looking forward to sitting down, putting my feet up, and taking a long, well-deserved sip of a chilled Chardonnay. That's when we heard a car door slam, followed by tires peeling out. Delaying my reward a moment longer, I peered out into the rain-streaked darkness. There in the middle of the street, likely anticipating a "good girl" followed by a treat from her owner, sat a well-trained puppy. Deserted. We did exactly what any fast-thinking family who had never owned a dog would do. We coaxed her out of the street and into our hearts with a path paved with American cheese. After a few phone calls to the Humane Society and visits to the vet, Molly became the newest member of our family.

Molly was a mutt who practically glowed in the sunlight. She had the golden coat of a Retriever, with a black aura, compliments of a healthy dose of German Shepherd. The night she adopted us was the night our family became complete. Molly was obsessed with a nubby blue ball she stole from the children next door. Using that ball, we could train her to do anything. Well, almost anything. As well-trained as she was, her favorite foods could cause her to cross the straight-

and-narrow to the naughty side. Molly's escapades are every bit as much a part of our family history as our children's first steps, prom dates, and wedding vows.

As a young mother with four children, putting a healthy dinner on the table night after night was an unwelcome chore. I would cook extra on the weekends to allow for a "leftover night" mid-week. This particular weekend, it was the family favorite, lasagna. Shortly before setting the table, my teenage daughter came home with half a dozen ravenous friends. Rather than crushing my leftovers plan, we walked to a local pizzeria. Before heading out, I pulled the lasagna from the oven, leaving it to cool while we were gone. That's when things got a little crazy.

We came home and loaded a movie into the DVR. Bedtime came and went. On leftovers night, I searched for the anticipated lasagna. It was nowhere. No one remembered putting it away. No one saw it. No one ate it. The pan was missing. The lasagna had vanished. Like any good mother, I looked from my husband to each child with a glare of accusation. Each looked back with the guilt-ridden eyes of someone who had used the "not me" excuse before and had been caught red-handed.

Fast forward a few months. It's a snowy early December day, and we are putting up our Christmas tree. Carols are playing, the kids are fighting over who gets to put the star on top. As we move the sofa from in front of the window to place the tree in its prominent position, I trip over – yes, a licked clean, long-forgotten lasagna pan! We look at Molly and recreate the Night of the Disappearing Lasagna from Molly's perspective.

Molly had been underfoot while I prepared the lasagna that day. Now and again, I would toss a piece of cheese across the floor to move her away. For an hour, she smelled dinner baking, thinking ahead to which child was most likely to slip her some of their dinner when I wasn't paying attention. She didn't understand why the plans changed or why the entire dinner was left for her. She just pulled it down from the stove and gorged herself. The whole thing. She cleaned the floor and the pan. As she ate it, the pan slid across the floor until it settled under the couch, there to stay for months. No one remembered her being sick or less hungry after the disappearance. Cold case solved!

While other dogs ran in their sleep, chasing rabbits in their dreams, I'm convinced Molly dreamt of stealing food in ever more elaborate ways. After the case of the missing lasagna, Molly never ate an entire dinner for six again, but she did continue her acts of devouring things you'd never expect. A bag of cough drops, including the wrappers. A package of mint candies, box and all! Molly had a knack for separating unsuspecting people from their dinner.

We were having one of those classic New England summer BBQs that starts early and ends long after the sun goes down, with everyone sitting around the fire pit. No one wanted to be the first to leave, afraid of breaking up the party. Rather than end the night, we fired up the grill for one more round of burgers. Molly had been perfect all day. She hadn't toppled any toddlers to steal their food or abscond with any unsupervised plates.

As a particular guest pontificated, using a medium rare cheeseburger in his left hand as a pointer to punctuate the importance of his words, the temptation was too great. Molly slinked in behind him, her golden hue less visible since sundown. Stealth wasn't an attribute bestowed on Molly often, and in this case, it probably had more to do with the evening's refreshments and less with the old girl's agility. Regardless, Molly found her way behind her victim, laser-focused on the dancing burger. When the burger came to rest, it was perfectly aligned with her watering mouth. In a single move, Molly managed to pull the prize from the bun, leaving her victim holding two slices of bread, none the wiser. Until his next bite. And by then, all evidence was gone, except a few giggling observers who watched the whole thing unwind.

Molly joined our family as a skittish innocent. She obediently accepted me as the alpha female and adamantly asserted her position over the children. If they took the fall for Molly's naughty behavior, she was fine with that.

Molly's final dinner was a ribeye steak, cooked rare, her favorite. She didn't eat much but enjoyed every morsel. That was nearly 15 years ago, and now the kids are grown with dogs of their own. Regardless, when we sit around enjoying a good meal, inevitably someone will say, "...remember when Molly would steal your dinner right out of your hand?"

Rest well, Molly dog!

My Dog Danced

– Donna Keefe –

On the back page of The Detroit Free Press arts section was a call for dogs to audition for a dance performance at the Detroit Music Hall. I thought it was odd and quite humorous, so I took my dog, Salem, who met the criteria for a small, black dog, to audition. I sat in the lobby set up for the dogs and their owners waiting for their turn to be interviewed.

Twenty-two dogs were waiting for an interview. As required by the news release, all were black, but not all were small. Some dogs looked like they were 50 to 60 pounds, with the white chest of tuxedo dogs. Others were dressed for the audition wearing bandanas and hats. One was wearing odd-looking socks. Sitting quietly with my undressed, small, black dog, I surveyed the group.

The three interviewers walked around quietly, observing the collection of canines hoping for their 15 minutes of fame. They approached the owners, sometimes asking questions, while at other times, and without much interaction, they sent away those who did not qualify. About 30 minutes passed while I watched the process and the elimination of the canine competition. Finally, an interviewer approached me and asked about the breed of my dog. After a few questions regarding her temperament, he then left the room. A short time later, the interviewer reappeared and told me we got the part in "Animal Trilogy." I was ecstatic and couldn't wait to tell everyone that my dog would be on stage in a dance performance in Detroit.

Salem was a Schipperke. This is a rare dog breed with a muscular, stocky build, weighing 20 to 30 pounds. They are curious, lively, intense little creatures that can also be mischievous. Bred in Belgium in the 1600s, their name is Flemish, meaning "little captain." They are classified as working dogs on the barges in the canals. I learned that it wasn't Salem's talent that got her the part but that she was the same breed as the founders of the Bill T. Jones/Arnie Zane Dance Company owned and performed with.

The show ran for two hours. At the end of the performance, Arnie Zane ran from the wings in front of the dancers and slid to center stage with Salem on a leash, standing proudly in front of him before the set went to black.

Salem and I were recognized in the program. She received a paycheck, and I got two comp tickets for each performance. It was exciting to be in the wings, watching the professional dancers concentrating on their timing and their movements from backstage. I had the opportunity to watch the show from the balcony with the lighting director and watched one performance seated in the audience. I felt strangely proud of my dog playing a critical role in "Animal Trilogy." Even though it only lasted five seconds at the very end, I sat grinning as she captured the audience by surprise.

It was an unusual and captivating performance; I had never seen one like it. Reading the reviews, I discovered it was a controversial dance company, one that exposed audiences to social issues that could be disturbing. I met Bill and Arnie there, who told me they could not travel with their dog and were thrilled when they heard a Schipperke was at the audition. We shared the special bond between dog owners, especially that of Schipperkes. I sheepishly asked if they would sign the program from each performance. Bill wrote, "Thanks, Salem," and Arnie added, "Long live the Schipperkes."

Arnie did not dance in the performance. His only appearance was at the end with Salem. He looked frail and wrapped himself in a blanket. I suspected he had AIDS. It was evident that Bill and Arnie were partners who built the dance company together, sharing their love for contemporary dance and each other. In 1987, they were ahead of their time in the current, modern dance world, with their choreography getting mixed reviews. I appreciated the different types of dancers and their athleticism, with men lifting men and women lifting men. The depth and meaning of each movement were unique, even for contemporary dance. The accompanying music, dialogue, and lighting were enthralling. After "Animal Trilogy," I followed news of them as they grew in popularity and became a well-known company for their bold, unconventional style and the significance of their performances.

Years later, living in Cambridge, Massachusetts, I saw that the Bill T. Jones/Arnie Zane Dance Company was coming to the Emerson Theater in Boston. By that time, Arnie had died of AIDS. I called the executive director of Dance Umbrella, the presenting organization, and asked if I could speak to Bill after the Friday night show. I told him the story of my dog performing with Bill and Arnie in Detroit. He asked me to find him at the theater with a note, which I did, and he would deliver it to Bill, which he did not.

I went to the show carrying my framed autographed copy of "Animal Trilogy," Salem's pay stub, and the articles from The Detroit Free Press. I intended to have Bill autograph the program for my collection. I wandered around the building, found the backstage entrance, and knocked on the door. I asked if I could speak with Bill and again mentioned that my dog performed with him at the Detroit Music Hall. They gave me a curious look, slightly skeptical of my story, and told me to wait.

To my surprise, Bill appeared. He remembered the show with my Schipperke. I felt a little silly standing at the door holding my program and pieces of a performance from the past. I conveyed how much I enjoyed the performance that night and was sorry about Arnie's passing. He was very gracious with his warm, gentle spirit and compassion.

I showed him my display of "Animal Trilogy" and asked for his autograph on the program. He stared at it as tears welled up in his eyes. There was a brief silence, then he quietly spoke, "Can I have this?" I was caught off guard by his request. I really didn't want to let go of my framed memory of Salem and the priceless event I shared with her. Telling me it was unique and he wanted it for the archives, I realized it meant more to him than to me. Bill thanked me for coming and bringing the program from "Animal Trilogy." As I relinquished my memories of Salem and Detroit to the Bill T. Jones/Arnie Zane archives, he autographed my program from that evening and wrote: "Dear Donna, Thanks for the memories."

Another Round of Nellie

– Ben Peterson –

On April 15th, 2013, I was up late, days after the horrific Boston Marathon bombing. I listened to the police scanner as our cities were captivated by the alarming manhunt for two Cambridge kids who decided to become murderers. I was scared and stressed and anxious. These anxieties were heightened when I learned the two suspects lived a very short dog walk away. After very little sleep, I drove to meet Nellie for the first time.

A few hours' ride west on Route 2, I pulled down a long dirt driveway into a grassy field blooming – not with flowers, but with Australian Shepherd puppies. I watched from a distance as one of these fuzzy little hedgehogs, with the hind-heavy musculature of the Bruins' Ray Bourque in his prime defensive years, corralled her sisters and brothers into order. As I got closer, her bright blue eyes looked back at me with the precision of a career Boston bartender; playful sarcasm, annoyance, and sincerity held in a delicate balance, "Can I help you?"

With her sibling herding complete, she eventually found her way to me. She gave an approving once-over, crawled up into my lap, and nuzzled her way into my wool coat. It was chilly for April. She nosed her way around my broken zipper – a not-so-subtle instruction to keep her warm. I followed her direction dutifully and folded my jacket around her. With one last heavy sigh, and a glance of deep empathy she must have honed in a former life of closing shifts behind the bar, she fell asleep. I fell in love. Her slow, deliberate breaths helped us both relax under the overcast of things happening around us.

She came home to Cambridge a few weeks later – and as any dog owner knows, she helped to turn small talk on the sidewalk into friendships. She helped to navigate new places, found secret routes to places to play, and scored treats. She's undeniably beautiful – her patchwork of copper, steel, and blue merle provided general cuteness relief for neighbors who had experienced turmoil and trauma in the aftermath of the Boston Marathon bombing. For several years, she shored up her position as queen, busy-body, and the narrator's most opinionated and most trusted personal confidant. She made a best friend in a docile (and probably impressionable) greyhound who lived next door. She received hand-drawn portraits from admiring neighbors. Principled to a fault, she became almost radically anti-skateboard but created a supportive bond with neighborhood kids amazed by her effortless athleticism in the sport of Frisbee. And then, quickly, without any warning, she became very sick.

In March of 2019, Nellie's relentless energy was notably dulled. She wasn't herself. She didn't look like herself. The insides of her ears, her skin, and her piercing blue eyes were overlaid with highlighter yellow. She was, without any earlier indication, dangerously jaundiced.

I spent more than a week making daily visits to see Nellie at Angell Memorial Hospital where doctors labored tirelessly to diagnose and relieve the life-threatening symptoms of a rare auto-immune disease with the tools and expertise reserved for the cutting edge of medicine. She looked like a cartoon poodle who'd run out halfway through one of their delicate canine topiary groomings. Her paws were poms, shaved at the ankles to administer IVs. The blaze of thick white fur between her torso and face was clear cut revealing a perfectly square patch of skin from where her blood was systematically withdrawn, cleaned, and transfused back into her body. The acrid, turmeric-yellow jaundice that pigmented her skin was present, but fading. Her blue eyes were tired. Without fail, and at every visit, she'd give an abundance of smooches and look back at me with the same unspoken retort: "Can I help you?" She was, and is, always working. This time, with the support and strength of her human doctors, survived.

Angell Animal Medical Center is a remarkable Boston institution. While I'm most immediately in greatest gratitude to the doctors at Angell who cared for Nellie, it's important to also acknowledge that we live in a city where care for our animal friends is as accessible, innovative, and life-saving as the world-renowned institutions that care for humans. The doctors at Angell saved Nellie's life. I'd like to think, maybe naively, that the way a city cares for its most vulnerable communities is an indication of its strength. Nellie is undoubtedly strong but is made stronger by the care of the doctors, neighbors, friends, and co-workers I'm lucky to share these cities with.

This year, Nellie turned 10. Ten whole years of adventuring. Ten years of immediate-icicle-on- fur-inducing swims in Maine. Ten years of butt-wiggling when her favorite human friends and family come to visit. Ten years after the violent events that terrorized our city in 2013 and what feels like a lifetime away from the day I found out I might lose her.

Today, with most of my time spent at home during the pandemic, Nellie's drive to work has found a more domestic and pedestrian outlet as my office manager. She'll take up residency under my feet at my desk or in front of my office door, ready for a task as duty calls. She frequently takes advantage of the employment perks of mid-day adventures in the Fells, the Blue Hills, or Fresh Pond.

Consider this a hymn and tribute to my gray Queen of Cambridge, who has never forgotten the home and family we created together in the wake of that terrifying day in April 10 years ago; the comfort and devotion she provided when everything seemed wrong, so fragile. Her glances remind me that this relationship has always been about helping each other understand that strength and resilience are rooted not only in hard work and perseverance but also in unwavering care. Nellie is indeed my faithful barkeep who waits for me to come through the door, wiping the counter clean as she greets me. "Can I help you? What's it going to be, Ben, the usual?"

It Started With Mr. Perkins

– Andrea Cleghorn –

In some families, dogs live long lives due to genes, good health care, and a safe, loving environment.

But in others, dogs aren't as lucky, as it sometimes takes people a while to figure out how to care for a pet. One family got the hang of this dog ownership thing with Tuffy, a Cairn Terrier, but that's after a few false starts.

So, let's go back to the beginning when Kay Coan and Andy Tobin were kids. Somewhere under a pile of photo albums in Massachusetts is a sepia-toned photograph in a round gold frame of a little girl. Kay, age 1, has sausage curls and is wearing a white dress, the toddler draped over an enormous Airedale. His name was Teddy, possibly for the first President Roosevelt. The photo was taken in the Northeast Kingdom of Vermont, circa 1921.

Borkin is only remembered through Andy's stories. A handsome black and tan "divil" with pointed ears, no one is around to verify this dog's name, either the spelling or the meaning. The best guess, since he was born into an Irish family new to this country, is that it came from John Patrick's pronunciation of the dog's annoying voice, as in "For God's sake, will ye stop the boyo's borkin, Brigid?" One of Andy's stories is that poor Brigid, his mother, was also blamed when the Tobin cat had kittens. Surely, the criticism bounced off her, what with wrangling six kids and keeping her firefighter husband busy with second and third jobs on his days off.

Kay and Andy grew up, coincidentally both went to school in the South and came back East after college. They went to work at General Electric, where they met and married after World War II. They had a baby and named her after Andy.

A few years later, Andy – probably thinking fondly of Borkin – talked his wife Kay into adopting a German Shepherd/Collie mix. Named Mr. Perkins – again, nobody knows why – the fluffball turned into a gigantic, energetic young dog. At this point, their daughter was 3 and they lived in a neighborhood packed with young kids. Perky enjoyed playing Bowling for Toddlers, and the consensus among the grownups was that the youngsters' lives were in peril, either to Perky's energetic jumping or an innocent sweep of his tail, which was the size of a Louisville Slugger.

The Tobins sent this lively fellow off to a farm just north of Hartford. (I can almost hear your skepticism, but no, they really did.) Mr. Perkins lived a long, happy life there with the chickens and fathered a son named Max. Their first child, the daughter mentioned above, was sent to the same farm at age 5 in anticipation of a second child's birth.

The difference was that Kay and Andy returned to retrieve their firstborn after Little Brother was born.

The family of four was bursting out of their West Hartford apartment when Andy started a new job in Manhattan. They bought the smallest house in Darien, Conn., and he commuted into the city. They looked at the house on a beautiful spring day, a Cape with a detached one-car garage. Somewhat mysteriously, they didn't see the inside of the garage – that door was locked. The realtor took Andy aside and offered to throw in the contents, at this point sight unseen but not unheard. He went along with it. "Why not?"

It was a loud garage because there was a Wire-haired Terrier inside.

Andy hooked a leash on Garage Dog and handed it to his 5-year-old daughter. G.D. needed a walk. He had a lot of pent-up energy and obviously no training on a leash. Picture this scene with its gravel driveway. The little girl was airborne, then dragged back and forth across the pebbles. She had tiny stones in her knees into her teen years.

So G.D. didn't last long, either.

But try, try again. The Tobins and the Murrays next door somehow happened upon a litter of Beagles. If anything is cuter than a black, tan, and white Beagle puppy, it is two Beagle puppies. So each family took one: Bootsie and Buddy.

Not much time was wasted on training, the yards weren't fenced, and when the neighborhood kids excitedly left home the first day of school, Bootsie and Buddy did too. The gang took off down the driveway (still gravel), down the hill to the end of the block where the forest began, through the big dark woods with a stream, over a small bridge, to the edge of the Baker School playground, and into the building. Of course, this daily 15-minute adventure was made much more fun with the addition of the pups. The administration was not amused, but, boy, the kids were. It happened more than once. One wonders where the mothers were – possibly inside with the three newborns between them. – when the gang took off on the mean streets of Darien to go to school with their two tiny service animals.

The pups' school days soon ended, but the Tobins' adventure in dog ownership continued. Kay reupholstered a wing chair while Bootsie enjoyed a crunchy lunch of upholstery tacks. The little dog passed through that adventure, but when she searched out and destroyed Kay's aqua lizigator slingbacks, it was literally all over for little Bootsie.

Decades later, Kay was asked by her grown-up daughter how she could euthanize a family pet for chewing a pair of shoes. "I didn't," she replied indignantly. "I took her to a shelter."

"And what did you think would happen to her there?" Was there a big market for a Beagle with a tummy full of tacks and fake leather shards in her teeth?

"I loved those shoes," she said.

Next up was a move to Chicago and a litter of Cairn Terriers. A small dog resembling Toto, Tuffy retained the name the breeder gave him and lived to old age and then some, at 17. He was a lackluster pet with the personality of a doormat. It wasn't that he was mean; he just didn't seem to care for the family members one way or the other.

Then Kay and Andy's daughter got married, moved to California, and around the time of the couple's third anniversary, they had the chance to adopt a dog. Shadow was from a Long Beach dog pound, as shelters were known then, initially by an inexperienced family that wasn't crazy about his catholic chewing habits...a refrigerator electrical cord, couch cushions, their son's Mr. Potato Head. The newlyweds went "just to take a look" and noticed that Shadow's worldly goods had already been packed up and were on the kitchen counter. The adoptive parents luckily were eager to take him in. The three of them got in the car and set off. He resembled a curly bear cub. They took him home and immediately renamed him Pooh for Winnie in the children's book.

Billed as a Cockapoo, the vet guessed Pooh was a Terrier/Poodle. He evolved from a black bear to a wooly gray Doodle, absolutely adored by everyone, none more than his two proud owners. Their newly purchased bicycles sat in the storage unit for a couple of years because where would Pooh ride – in a basket? They took him to UCLA and Santa Monica Pier. They went to Zuma Beach in Malibu all year round, Pooh occasionally lifting his leg on innocent people reclining in their beach chairs.

Pooh loved everybody indiscriminately. The family joke was if there was ever a divorce and the judge asked Pooh to pick a custodial parent; he would go home with the bailiff. It was a good life for him, with road trips up and down the California coast, teetering on the edge of the Grand Canyon on one cross-country trip in a VW bug, and racking up more airline miles than 99 percent of Americans.

When the owners went back-packing to Europe for an extended stay a few years later, Pooh was farmed out to close family friends in West Los Angeles. There he lived with a loving gang of teenagers, got to hang out with Donnie and Marie Osmond, and had his fill of pizza and ice cream that packed 10 pounds onto his slender 25-pound frame.

After the humans' transatlantic sojourn, Pooh was returned to his family, now living in Boston. He enjoyed the Bicentennial on Boston Common and went to his first, but hardly last, Marathon.

Pooh went on to live a rich Beantown life, ending the Curse of the Tobins.

Molly's Lair

– Len Charney –

It was clear that Molly was hellbent on delivering her litter with no one else around when she slipped away from the cabin in the days leading up to their birth. Though not even 2 years old, she had become particularly self-reliant, at times aloof, preferring to adjust to changes on her own terms.

My friend Kevin and I adopted Molly from the Ithaca Animal Shelter our junior year at Cornell in the fall of 1969. She was 8 weeks old, a handsome German Shepherd/Black Lab mix, with thick sable fur, pointy ears that stood at attention – at times rotating individually to pinpoint faint distant sounds – and intense brown eyes that saw through everything.

Molly came into her own quickly, taking full advantage of her autonomy on Cornell's dog-friendly campus. After a very brief period of sleeping peacefully at our feet during class, she flourished socializing with packs of like-minded canines on the sprawling campus. I grew accustomed to the sound of her clanging collar and distinctive pitter-patter gait, sniffing her way down echoing corridors to make countless uninvited class appearances, or eventually finding her way back to either of our apartments after a day of exploring. She was totally comfortable out in nature, an intrepid companion on day hikes and extended outings, regardless of the weather or precarious terrain.

She became even more independent when we moved to Slaterville Springs, a rural hamlet southeast of Ithaca where we formed an eclectic compound. It was made up of a modest cabin where Kevin and his girlfriend Chris lived, my one-room yurt camouflaged against a forested backdrop. A repurposed caboose, used as a plow car, had been hauled up two years earlier from Ithaca's railyards by another Cornell itinerant. These dwellings branched out from an inclined clearing that emptied into Six Mill Creek, a 20-mile, glacially-etched channel characterized by steep gorges, a string of abandoned mill sites, and a pristine watershed that supplies Ithaca's drinking water to this day.

Molly was never more content than the two years we lived there, whether bounding across goldenrod meadows, pecking at brook trout and shiners in the gravelly creek bed, often patiently crouched like a stalking wolf. She was feral and free-spirited, a delight to watch in action. She frequently scratched at the door to present her latest prey or live catch wriggling in her closed jaws. Only once did she return in terrible pain with a half dozen porcupine quills embedded in her inflamed muzzle.

Molly kept up her gallivanting during most of her pregnancy. It was only the final week that she became noticeably distressed, requiring more sleep and expending great effort to move about with her bloated belly. Nonetheless, she would not stand for being confined indoors, something our local veterinarian had advised we try when he stopped by the weekend before she gave birth. "Knowing Molly," he acknowledged as he placed his stethoscope back in his bag, "she's likely to bolt. Better make sure she stays close and maintain a watchful eye."

We tried attaching a 50-foot line to Molly's collar, but she barked nonstop, and we released her for our sanity. She behaved for less than a day, waiting until we were out of her line of sight before taking off. Realizing she had gone missing, we split up, moving along the creek and searching the nearby woods, calling her name to no avail. She finally reappeared hours later, to our great relief, but horrified by her dreadful appearance. Her normally glistening fur was matted with a thick layer of mud, her nose was caked – imagine a doggie facial – and her encrusted paws resembled worn combat boots. We soaked her gently with warm water in a galvanized metal trough. Following a brief period of calm after being dried off, she became agitated and unsettled, whining uncharacteristically and moving restlessly about from one spot to another.

Her anxiety filled the cabin, heightened by a dramatic worsening of the weather. Within a matter of minutes, the late afternoon sky darkened from a thick blanket of menacing clouds until the smothered sun disappeared completely. The temperature dropped sharply and stiff gusts of wind preceded torrential rain moving in from the north. I stayed on for dinner, hoping the storm would pass, but conditions only deteriorated further. I managed the 400-foot walk to the yurt, stoked the fire, and settled in for the night. Kevin knocked on my door around 11 to report that Molly had once again escaped. Neither he nor Chris had a clue about how she nudged the door open, or why they had not heard it slam shut.

I grabbed my rain slicker, pulled on my rubber waders, and collected the large Coleman gas lantern. Kevin instinctively emptied a slatted bushel basket of seasoned firewood beside the stove, gripping it by the wire handle as we flew out the door. We headed to the edge of the clearing and stepped into the creek, zigzagging between opposing banks, edging upstream, startled by how unmanageable the current had become in only a matter of a few hours. We suspected we were witnessing the initial stages of what neighbors had described as the beginnings of flash floods when scores of small streams deposited an unimaginable volume of water to erode or even breach the banks of this otherwise tranquil stretch of the creek.

We had not gone very far – it was hard to gauge the distance because our progress was so slow – when Kevin stopped abruptly, clutched my arm, and motioned: "Listen, do you hear that?" I directed the hissing lantern to the adjacent bank where we heard an almost indiscernible series of faint, low-pitched groans. Molly emerged from what appeared to be a carved hollow tunnel a couple of feet above the base of the creek. She glowered motionless with gnashing teeth and let out the most chilling growl I had ever heard.

We stepped forward cautiously, repeating her name gently while getting our first close look at her crude lair, surmising this was the result of her previous day's digging. At the very back of the makeshift den, we made out four brand-new puppies with their eyes shut, famished, and distraught by their mother's sudden departure. The water had risen high enough in the creek to begin seeping beyond the lip of the cavity, already prompting Molly to move the pups as far back as she could to protect them from possible harm.

There was a brief pause in the storm, perhaps giving Molly time to recognize the perilous situation her newborns were in. She retreated to the back of the shallow cave and gently enveloped the pups in her mouth, one at a time, lowering them reluctantly into our outstretched, cupped hands. We placed them in the slatted basket; I removed my slicker to cover them as carefully as possible. We each clasped a wire handle and moved single-file along the edge of the bank, where the turbulent water made it difficult to maintain our footing. We came to a bend in the channel and located a spot where the slope of the embankment was reasonable enough to inch ourselves to higher ground. We forged ahead slowly, eventually stepping onto the narrow, well-trodden path we knew. Miraculously, Molly had been able to maintain our painstaking pace, nuzzling her head in the basket from time to time and licking her babies protectively until we were safely back at the cabin. We dried them under Molly's guarded scrutiny, placing blankets and pillows to form a bed for her to lie with her fragile brood, grateful that the ordeal was over.

It has been a long time since I last thought about the events surrounding the birth of Molly's only litter 52 years ago. I have never forgotten her agonizing confusion and sadness when it came time for her to forfeit her offspring to an assortment of friends and strangers. How she struggled to fully forgive or trust me again.

Advance the clock several years to one more adjustment that Molly was asked to make. She became my mom's full-time companion and service dog after Dad passed away, a role she assumed for the remainder of her life.

Dutiful and devoted as ever, always shouldering change with uncommon grace and dignity, Molly's was a life of understated resiliency and perseverance. She offered up splendid examples time and again.

My Hero, the Amazing Maisie

– Emeline Lo-Piliero –

There are lots of reasons Maisie is my hero. Here are a few of them.

First, she is a compassionate dog who always knows when you're in trouble. For example, she sat by my side for hours when I was upset. When I am sad Maisie always makes me smile with some of her tricks.

Second of all, she is a loyal canine who is willing to save you at the cost of her life. For instance, on one walk we met up with a coyote lingering on the street. She scared it away by barking, at the price of one of us getting injured. Maisie makes a lot of noise to warn us when she sees any passersby – humans, cars, or trucks.

Lastly, she is an affection-seeker and an affection-giver.

Maisie nuzzles my side all the time and wagging her tail is one of her many adorable traits. She licks me whenever she sees me and barrels into me licking enthusiastically, giving doggie kisses to me and her loved ones.

Last but not least, she gives me a love nudge – for food, affection, or toys. As you can see, Maisie is a compassionate, loyal, and affectionate dog who will always be by your side when you need her.

ASSIGNMENT MY HERO BY EMELINE LO-PILIERO, AGE 8

A Dog: The Best Pet to Get!

– Cooper Ogden –

I get off the bus, say hi to my mom, and my wonderful pups Cesar and Puchi greet me by begging me for pats and sniffing me – it tickles! I walk into the kitchen to get myself a snack but my dogs start sniffing me, so I get them a treat. They are so cute! I think dogs are the best pets because they are super cuddly, they can help the police, and they can keep you healthy. Can your cat do any of that?!

The first reason dogs are the best pets is because they are cuddly. For example, my dogs love it when I cuddle them. It is super fun to pat them because they can sometimes be very soft. Cesar has silly hair that sometimes we can shape to look like a unicorn in the front! And sometimes they can climb over you, and it is hilarious! I can cuddle them anytime. When I am sad, Cesar comes over and lets me pat him. As you can see, dogs are super cuddly!

Another reason a dog is the best pet is because they can help the police. For example, they can sniff out bombs that people might try to explode or drugs that a person might be carrying. Another example is that they can find missing people who might be buried in debris, who cannot breathe or are probably unconscious. Puchi is not a police dog, but she likes to guard our family by sitting near us outside.

The final reason a dog is the best pet is because they can keep you healthy. For instance, a dog can keep you off the couch. Sometimes, I am on the couch, and Cesar gets me to play fetch and tug of war. The funny thing is, he only plays fetch indoors, never outside! In addition, dogs can go for walks and that can keep you super healthy. Now you can see why dogs can do so much... unlike cats!

In conclusion, dogs are cuddly, they can help the police, and they can keep you healthy. Dogs will cuddle you anytime, dogs can make you feel better when you are sad, and they are even willing to play fetch. If you are looking for an awesome pet, then you should definitely get a dog!

We Love Our Buckethead

– Laura Wals –

As long as I can remember, I always wanted a dog at our home in the Netherlands. My parents finally agreed since they were working remotely during the pandemic. We started looking at shelters to find a dog that needed a home. My aunt volunteers at dog shelters on the island of Bonaire – in the Caribbean – which is part of the Kingdom of the Netherlands. She started to keep an eye out for us and one day sent a picture of a little dog about 5 years old that had just been rescued from living on the streets. At the shelter, they had named her Snowy because she sheds like crazy and it looks like falling snow. We didn't know her original name or how she ended up living on the streets. Eventually, we renamed her Kaya. Kaya means street in Papiamentu, the native language of Bonaire. She is still "snowy," though, when we pet her.

Kaya had to take a very long plane ride to get to where we live. She arrived on the morning of Dec. 30, 2020. She was very scared and didn't understand what was going on. I think because she really likes kids, she was very happy to see me. We sat together for a long time that first day.

Kaya's ears flap up and down when she walks, and when she looks up at you, they stick straight up. She has a heart-shaped face, beautiful brown eyes, and a cute button nose like me, and you can see her two little crooked bottom teeth when she smiles. One side of her face is white, and the other side is brown. Her eyelashes match in color on each side. Her body is mostly white with light brown speckles. We think she is a Jack Russell and Beagle mix. Her tail curls up at the end, with a little bit of brown, but is mostly white as snow. Since she likes to beg, her tail is always in action asking for treats or wanting her belly rubbed. She keeps her paws very clean, but we have to clean off her eye boogers.

Kaya doesn't like toys very much, but she loves food. Before she arrived, we bought a lot of toys, but she only liked the ones with food in them. She gets very happy at feeding time and runs and jumps all around until we tell her to sit on her mat to calm her down. She has to stay there until we put the food down and say "OK!" It's always funny then because the mat goes flying in the opposite direction when she takes off running to eat. Kaya especially likes visiting my grandma because she gets treats.

I keep teaching Kaya new tricks. Sometimes, Kaya is a ballerina on her tippy toes or jumping over my legs. Other times she sits on her butt like a bear to get a treat. She loves to run with me. It took time for me to teach her that it's OK to be picked up. She trusts me most of the time. She has even trusted me enough to sit on my skateboard, but only a couple of times. Kaya can sense when it's bath time, though. When you walk up to her anywhere near the bathroom, she immediately rolls on her back, making it harder to pick her up. She's very smart.

We have multiple names for Kaya now: Kaya, KayKay, Babushka, Schatje Patatje, Booger, and, if she's being ornery, Buckethead.

My favorite time is when Kaya can sleep in my room at night. We share a language. I know what she's thinking, and she knows what I'm saying. I give her kisses, we cuddle and "talk." She knows my secrets and keeps them safe.

Waiting for Scout

– Kate Cotter –

The day I moved into my freshman dorm, my stomach was so clenched I could barely breathe, my nerves so heightened that my hands shook. The dorm was named Little because it was. Some of those "little kids," as we called ourselves, became my people quickly, easily, and deeply. We spent many evenings that first year talking into the night, listening to music, laughing, crying, sometimes under the influence of a substance, sometimes under the influence of hormones, and occasionally actually doing schoolwork.

Six of us from freshman year, more than two decades after graduation, meet yearly for a reunion weekend if only to be together and remember those moments that helped to carve our smiles, our paths, and our lives so far. This particular year, we decided to meet at Cindy's new home.

During the few weeks leading up to our reunion weekend, unusual things were happening in my house. It started with a flickering light in my kitchen. I changed the bulb; still, it flickered. Then, I started waking up every night at 3 a.m., feeling an energy I didn't recognize.

One night, I felt Kona, my sweet husky mutt, touch his nose to the small of my back. I startled and rolled over to pet him, but Kona was not there. I got out of bed to look for him and found him sleeping...downstairs. He had never been in the room at all. And that's when it became clear to me: someone, or something, was trying to get my attention.

That meant I then had to talk to my friend Leslie. Leslie and I have often discussed the spirit world and our experiences with it. But Leslie can read more, knows more, and has seen more. So, as I set off on my drive for the reunion, I called Leslie. She listened and knew the right questions to ask.

"You're in the car," she said. "Where are you going?"

"To my friend Cindy's house," I told her.

"OK, and who is connected to Cindy?"

Oh. The air left my lungs.

Doug. I met Doug back on that first day of college as my mother and I trudged up and down the stairwell in the August humidity. We carried boxes, twinkle lights, and a tiny fridge. We passed Doug and his parents so many times that we all finally introduced ourselves. Doug had a mop of light brown curls, a side smile, and a baseball cap; he fit the part of the New England college kid to a T. Doug's mother wasn't carrying any boxes. She wore a skirt and suit jacket, pearls, and a tight gray bun. As our mothers talked, Doug was instantly generous with his kindness: he asked where I was from, we joked about private school, and he said he had an extra fan if we needed to cool off our room. I liked him right away.

I learned that Doug had come to college straight from boarding school. He was used to dorm life and knew exactly how to set up his tiny, single room – a tapestry on the long wall, soft lighting, cinder blocks to loft his bed, and mounted stereo speakers. He had it down to a science, complete with an espresso machine and all the prescription Adderall he could snort. Which he did, sometimes too much. And if you caught him with a blue ring around his nostril, he'd shrug it off with that half-smile he used constantly, as if he would only let a part of himself tell the truth.

During that first year, Doug also met Cindy. They were one of those college pairs that solidified quickly, and their names became synonymous: Doug and Cindy, Cindy and Doug. After college, they went to business school, each becoming an incredible success individually and together. In our 30s, when I heard they broke up, I was sad but not very surprised. Doug was, honestly, a difficult person to love. But Cindy and Doug never lost sight of each other, even after they said goodbye. They looked in on each other with those distance binoculars that love builds over time.

And then, on an October night in 2017, my phone rang. Doug had taken his own life.

I told Leslie all of this as I drove to Cindy's house. She and I agreed: this could be Doug trying to communicate. "Tonight, invite the message out loud before you go to sleep," Leslie told me. "Tell him to say what he needs to say. Tell him you'll listen."

As I pulled up to Cindy's house, her stately brindle pup, Tonka, was waiting outside like a garden statue on the front step. He greeted me politely, his sleek sides wiggling like a tall fish, mirroring how I felt to see my friends. We spent our evening together, talking, and I told my friends everything that had been happening in my home. I also told them about my instructions from Leslie. We headed off to sleep in the early hours of the morning.

I laid on my air mattress and said, out loud into the darkness: "I'm here–send me your message. I'll pass it on." And I slept.

In the morning, I found Cindy outside, throwing the ball for Tonka. The air sat quietly over the yard, fog hovering over the pond. No one else was awake yet. I did have a dream early that morning, in that space between asleep and awake, but I was completely unsure if it meant anything at all. So outside, both of us barefoot on the driveway, I told Cindy about my dream.

I dreamed of a bright green field, rolling hills, and blue skies.

In front of me arrived a black dog, shaggy and happy; he looked like a black golden retriever. He was leaping, playing with a blotchy-colored dog with no tail. I asked them their names, and they said Moby and Scout. As I watched them frolic, I felt a sharp pin-prick feeling in my thumb, and I kept pressing my pointer finger against it to stop the pain. I realized I was pressing my fingers together to make the "OK" sign. Asleep, I looked at my fingers, looked back at the dogs, and woke up.

I looked at Cindy, whose arms had fallen to her sides, her eyes wide. "That's my dog," she said. "Our dog. Moby was our dog." And my eyes filled with tears. We held each other and then Cindy showed me a picture of the exact black dog from my dream. His fur, his face: identical.

Her smile was so bright as she spoke about her pup, their child together. She said it made sense that Doug would communicate through Moby, almost hiding behind him. She sat quietly and then said, "He's OK. I just wanted him to be OK."

When everyone else was awake, we started to go through the details. The big question: who was Scout? We all had dogs and grew up with dogs, but Scout, this colorful dog with no tail, none of us knew. We even reached out to Doug's sister to see if there was a Scout in the past. But no one could place Scout.

We went on a hike, a strange calm energy pushing us forward, a contentedness filling my chest. And when it was time to go, I felt like I was leaving a memory that we could hold and think about whenever we needed to. I called Leslie on my drive home. I told her about Moby, thanking her for the advice, finishing with how we hadn't yet figured out the mystery of Scout.

"Remember," Leslie reminded me, "the spirit world doesn't have the notion of time or place. Maybe Scout hasn't been here, yet."

A smile poured across my face. Scout could be coming to Cindy sometime in the future. And for now, he's busy playing with Moby. And probably Doug. I can see Doug chuckling, knowing his message brought relief and comfort. And until the next reunion weekend, my college friends – every single one of us – are surrounded by our pups and their soft noses poking us gently in the right direction, content in the knowledge that we are all OK as we wait for Scout to come.

Are Dogs Just Studying Us?

– Gene Kalb –

Maybe it's just my being suspicious, but do you ever have the feeling you're being tested by your dog? I don't mean being tested like a toddler tests a parent. Dogs are not necessarily looking for limits, but they are really trying to see what we as humans, are capable of learning. This seems to be more than a few individual canines having fun, as there appears to be a big deep conspiracy to gather information on humans' ability to learn. The reasons why are not clear, but should we be scared?

Take our dog for example. We have a 98-pound Black Lab/mix rescue dog who I swear has a clipboard hidden somewhere in our house where he is recording his experiments on us. For example, every time we sit down for dinner he goes to the door and appears to want to go out. He rarely if ever actually goes out, as it seems his goal is to see how many times he can get me to open the door. There was a New Yorker cartoon recently of a dog dressed in a tuxedo with the caption of the wife saying, "Howard, I think the dog wants to go out."

"Howarding" has become a verb in our house. For the record,

I have opened the door 758 times, with the actual threshold being crossed a couple dozen times. Clearly, he is testing the intermittent reward theory.

Our dog also seems to have a sense of humor about where he does his business. Having learned that for whatever reason, humans like to collect dog poop and bring it home, he has embarked on what can only be called a series of experiments on "how bad does he want it?" My retrieval efforts have included climbing to the top of an 8-foot-high snowbank, reaching through a wire fence, and getting stuck on a blackberry bush, to name just a few. Keep in mind none of those particular locations were necessary for him to complete his task. It was more of a challenge to me, and apparently he loves a challenge.

If our dog is working on his bachelor's, we have friends with a dog who is working on her Ph.D. dissertation. Their smaller Black Lab has perfected the art of the stare. She will just stare at you to the point that you start asking her questions. (Hint: When you start asking your dog questions, you lose.) What do you want? Do you need to go out? Surprisingly, you never get an answer. I swear this dog has a stopwatch running to see how long it will take to get that treat. Her evening ritual now involves carrots, parmesan cheese (imported), blueberries, and yogurt, I'm sorry Greek yogurt, mind you, and items of interest from several food groups. There is a certain smugness to her that suggests this is all just a game, and she's winning.

I hear similar stories from other friends with their dogs. You can't help but think this is some kind of coordinated effort on the part of some canine overlord out there. For example, think about how the world of dog training (dog training – ha!) has changed. Years ago it was always about the owner being dominant, the leader of the pack. "Be consistent and firm" was the mantra. The current guidance seems to be to give the dog a treat for any behavior you want to encourage. Sit, come, stay, lie down, stand up, go, don't go, stop, bark, don't bark, paw, use your indoor voice. It is all to be rewarded with a treat.

Do you really believe there wasn't a master plan for all this to be accomplished? Whoever it is who's calling the shots, they're brilliant!

Lost and Found

– Brenda Riddell –

He was a small pup with big ears, scruffy white fur, and a long, curly tail. His appearance earned him the name Bolt at the shelter after the animated dog in the movie of the same name. My husband Ken and I first saw his picture in the adoptable dogs section of the shelter website in February 2017. He was only 5 months old and fresh off the plane after his rescue from the streets of Puerto Rico. He had been a lost puppy, blessed to be among the few homeless dogs on the island to get a second chance at a better life.

Ken and I had been thinking of getting a dog for a while. We were at a time in our lives where we were – for whatever reason – spending less time out with friends and more time at home. So, we knew we'd appreciate the companionship of a dog. We looked at rescue and shelter websites for a few months to get an idea of the type of dog we'd want to adopt to fit into our lifestyle. We knew we preferred a small- to medium-sized dog, but we weren't too particular about the breed.

And then, one day, Bolt popped up in one of our searches. Of course, it's difficult to tell how large a rescue dog will be without knowing his entire lineage, but we had a hunch from his "Westie mix" label that he'd fit our size requirement. Then we saw that little white scruffy face – well, we immediately fell in love. We decided to inquire with the shelter. One problem: We were starting our last day of vacation in Florida, and the dog, seemingly beckoning us through that photo, was in Massachusetts.

We visited the shelter the very next morning after our flight home. Anxious to find out if Bolt was still there, we arrived 15 minutes before they opened and waited for the volunteer staff to let us in. Once inside, the kennel area overflowed with dogs of all ages and sizes. Some were nervous and shy, while others were excited or loud. But one thing was for sure – there wasn't much room for more. It hit home that this is just one shelter facility in a small city. I couldn't help but wonder what the situation was like nationwide.

Bolt spotted us, immediately trotting up to the front of the kennel to get a better look. He was spunky and seemingly excited to see new faces. We watched as he patiently waited for the shelter volunteer to take him out of the kennel, wagging his tail but sitting quite still as if to say, "See, I'm a good boy." We took him outside in their fenced-in yard to see how he'd react to us without other animals nearby. He freely approached both of us with little to no coaxing. It seemed he was, indeed, a good boy. The interaction between us was natural. So, we did what we first set out to do. We took him home.

We introduced Bolt to my mom, my brother, and our nephew right away. Even though he was a bit shy at first, he acclimated to our home and eventually settled into our family. His name, however, sounded a bit harsh to us. So, we all agreed it needed to be changed. Through Facebook, we solicited our friends and family for names. We tossed around the names Petey or Pedro, an homage to a few of our favorite Boston Red Sox players. Then, a cousin suggested the name Otto, and it stuck. The dog somehow just looked like an Otto.

The first month of dog ownership had its share of challenges. Our pup got sick a few times, and subsequently, we quickly got to know our veterinarian. He also immediately disliked our neighbor's dog, losing his cool whenever he spotted the innocent Black Lab through the fence that divides our properties. However, these things were fixable. Challenges aside, he filled our house with life, activity, and happiness.

I always liked the idea of having an office dog to break up a daily work routine. I imagined organizing healthy breaks to take walks or play fetch. My coworkers, all pet parents, agreed that having a pup around could boost morale. So, after a few months of obedience training, I felt confident enough to start bringing Otto to my office in downtown Portsmouth, N.H.

Ken joined us at the office on one particularly sunny and warm April day. Since adopting Otto, we became familiar with the ongoing demands of a puppy bladder. We found it challenging during work hours to keep running the dog down flights of stairs into the middle of downtown to do his thing. During one potty break, I got lazy and didn't put Otto's harness on him before heading outside. Even though we decided to change the dog's name to Otto, we didn't find out how appropriate the name Bolt really was until that moment.

It took mere seconds for Otto to wriggle out of his collar after getting spooked by a car horn right outside my office. I was utterly horrified as off he went, running in and out of traffic in a major downtown intersection. Well-meaning bystanders tried to catch him, but that only frightened him more. Ken flew into action when he heard my desperate screams from the office, pleading with Otto to come back. Otto went into full flight mode, sprinting down Market Street toward the iconic salt stockpiles that greet you as you enter the city. Boy, that dog really turned on the jets. Ken took off after him. I stood there frozen, empty collar and leash in hand, not knowing what to do next.

Otto ran all the way to those salt piles, about a quarter mile away from my office, as Ken trailed behind. The road went on for miles, and if he continued running straight ahead, it was unlikely that Ken would catch him. Thankfully, Otto turned right into a parking lot and hid behind a dumpster. Ken was able to carefully approach and scoop him up. Cradling Otto in his arms, he slowly walked back up Market Street to the cheers and claps of worried bystanders.

After that incident, we learned to keep Otto well-protected on walks. I purchased a strong harness and a leash with a heavy-duty carabiner connection. They remain a constant reminder of how close we were to losing Otto that day.

Going through the adoption process and walking through that shelter opened my eyes to the animal homelessness crisis. It also sparked in me a desire to help. After speaking with several local rescues, I got hooked on raising awareness about homeless and lost animals. I started volunteering for several rescues and drew upon my background in marketing and design to promote others working in animal advocacy.

After sharing countless stories about adoptable or lost dogs on social media, my family and friends thought I was becoming a bit obsessed. I think I simply found an earnest sense of purpose. Thank you, Otto, for getting lost in Puerto Rico so I could find you and a little piece of myself. But let's not get lost again, OK? Good boy.

Adorable Psychopath

– Helen Morse –

Rita the Chihuahua tagged along whenever Aunt Ida came to our house. The moment Rita stepped in the door, she was all about my mother. While Mom and Ida greeted each other, Rita danced and pranced at my mother's ankles, frantically wagging her tiny tail and fawning, doing everything she could to get Mom to pick her up. She was always successful.

Of course, our Pekinese Pitapat was unimpressed. She was right there to answer the door, half excited, doing her languid crooning howl only to wander away once she saw who it was. Pitapat was more perplexed than anything by the guest dog's outrageous display. All that fussing, and for what? Pitapat was an easygoing soul; she may not have been the brightest bulb on the tree, but she was affable. She didn't care if she was sitting at your feet or on your lap. Either way was all right, and when you put her down, that was fine, too. She would go on her way with no hard feelings.

Pitty's heavy coat was long, cottony, and easily matted, and she walked with a lumbering gait. If she had been human, she would have been a short but "big-boned" girl with enormous, kind eyes beneath a mop of hair badly in need of professional attention. Her taste in clothes would have been on the dowdy side, and she would have been an absent-minded and eccentric optimist who was affectionate in the extreme. No doubt, her friends would have loved her for all those qualities. Pitty moved with a cloud of fur that would cling to our clothes. But she doled out her affection freely, without keeping score, and my two sisters and I adored her.

Rita was her opposite. She had eyes only for my mother. Intelligent, calculating, nervous, and paranoid, Rita's good graces were tough to win and most often temporary. In human form, she would have been a neat and stylish loner. She would have been vain, favoring Chanel outfits and sharp little custom-made hats ordered from Paris, which she would wear artfully tipped over one eye. She would have been fabulously pretty with a jealous streak that was like jet fuel for her paranoia while she compared herself to everyone else. But for us kids, Rita was an utter fascination – an irresistible attraction.

Mostly black with tan accessories, she had tight and glossy fur, large expressive brown eyes, and perky ears that were delicate and slightly oversized. She looked cuddly, but her appearance was deceptive – so deceptive, in fact, that we never quite learned to stay away from her, even after we knew better. Rita's displays of sweetness were a strange curse, luring us in and making us think that maybe – just maybe – things would be different this time. As cute as she was, as charming as she could be with Aunt Ida and our mother, with us, she was vicious – a pint-sized psychopath.

Once we settled into the living room, with my mother in one corner of the couch and Ida beside her at the other end, Rita would sit in our mother's lap like a tiny elegant queen upon a larger one. She surveyed her kingdom from beneath our mother's casual but loving hand. Rita nestled in, reflexively licking her perfect Chihuahua lips, having scored the throne, the best seat in the house. She was prepared to guard it too, with whatever means necessary. To this end, her eyes darted back and forth at the rest of us, ever watchful that no one dared disturb her position.

Rita kissed our mother's loving fingers while she kept her eyes on all of us as if to say, "Look at me! I can do this, and you can't!" Eventually, she would relax, and what followed never varied. She would lay her muzzle down on our mother's knee, take a deep breath, and snuffle in, satisfied that her claim was secure. That was when one of us would ask Mom if it was a good time to pet her. We knew it was our best chance, with our mother's soothing voice above her, "Good girl, Rita, such a good girl..." We could tentatively extend a hand and gently smooth her soft brow, running our adoring fingers from across her neck and toward her shoulder. We were not to touch her anywhere else because we already knew she didn't like it. Mom could touch her anywhere. We could not.

Most of the time, this strategy worked well enough, but not always, and that was the problem. We had to observe Rita carefully for any sign of warning. It would start with her shifting her focus from us to some imaginary far horizon. Then, she would get so still it brought to mind the calm preceding a storm. The effort to change her demeanor made her shake ever so slightly; then she stopped blinking. Although her eyes were already slightly prominent, at this point, they seemed to emerge from her head just a millimeter more in the tension of the moment.

At some unknown time, many minutes earlier, she had decided that our time was up, and a tiny rumbling in her throat would begin to sound. At this point, the only thing we could think was a panicked, "Get out of the way – NOW!" But we knew if we had any chance at all, it was essential not to startle Rita by moving our small hands away too fast.

It was by then too late. We may as well have extended our fingers into a wood chipper. She wasn't thinking anymore, and neither were we. We tried to remove the offending hand as unobtrusively as possible, but that ship had sailed. It didn't matter how or when we withdrew our hands; it was inevitable that her teeth and our fingers would soon meet. The explosion came in a blizzard of vocal objection and audible jaw-snapping, and Rita landed as many nips as she could in a rapid-fire frenzy.

As we jumped backward from the little spitfire, our already-bristling mother turned on her offspring. "You see? When will you learn?! I told you she doesn't always like to be petted. That's what you get!" Then, soothing the savage beast, she would coo, "Poor Rita, sweet Rita! There, there, it's OK, it's OK," while smoothing the hackles that had risen around her neck and down her spine. Rita would lick her lips with a grimace a few times as if trying to remove a bitter taste from her mouth, and then just as quickly, she would settle back down in Mom's lap, accepting her apologies as one royal to another. To us, they appeared to be two like-minded creatures.

It was many visits and some years later that Aunt Ida arrived at the house one afternoon: Alone, heartbroken, and inconsolable. She had come to share with our mother the terrible news of Rita's passing. Although we felt sorry for Aunt Ida, and even for Rita herself, I confess while Ida wept with Mom on the couch, we excused ourselves and ran to the playroom to avoid being caught with the smiles creeping onto our faces.

Hearing the hubbub, Pitapat followed us. We could see that she felt curious about whatever it was that had us all in an uproar. And we knew, in her way, she was ready and willing to offer us her kind condolences. But we wondered too, if she might have had just the tiniest bit of self-satisfaction after all, for being the true top dog she was.

For our part, we were sorry that Rita and the temptation of Rita was now gone, even though we had failed to befriend our adorable, irresistible, and crazy little visitor.

Did we regret the drama and the danger?

No.

She was totally worth it.

The Fate of Spot and Smudge

– Robert Udulutch –

What if my boss hadn't made me work that Saturday? I wouldn't have been in a snarly mood, and I wouldn't have been a complete ogre to my girlfriend. She was pouting because she had one of her 'cute' days all planned out for us, and I had grumbled that her cute plans were worse than working, even though I knew she just wanted to spend some time together.

We traded immature barbs before I stomped out of our apartment, and then I took the longest possible route to the office to cool off. I also added a stop for a rare impulse donut, and chose to go inside instead of driving-thru even though the place was jamming and I abhor waiting in lines.

That put me in the queue behind a perky chatty couple, where I overheard them planning their annoyingly cute Saturday together, which included some fun bargain hunting at a local craft fair.

Normally my ears wouldn't have pricked up about a clutter fair, but taking my miffed sweetheart for some cheesy bargain hunting after work might just smooth things over.

Especially because she loved that kinda junk, and she knew I hated that kinda junk.

But my plan to rescue our cute day fell apart when we got to the fair later that afternoon to find most of the booths were closing. The unsold handicrafts and artisan honeys and not-so-great beachy landscape paintings with seagulls that looked more like chickens were being packed away, and she accused me of having worked late on purpose so we'd miss the good useless stuff.

She paused at a scrappy booth to poke through a stack of used books, and while she continued to carp at me she picked out a children's book about a puppy named Spot.

It had pop-up pages, and she said I should get it for my nephew's upcoming birthday, adding that I'd probably miss his party because I'd probably have to work.

She moved on to a booth with stupidly overpriced craft soaps, where she smelled each little bar and griped about having missed the better soaps, whatever that meant.

If she hadn't whined in that certain grating way that plucked at my last patient nerve I wouldn't have rolled my eyes, and I wouldn't have hunted for anything to look at other than her pinched damning face.

So I wouldn't have turned to the next booth, which displayed a few dozen paintings of horse faces that were kinda creepy, and I wouldn't have looked away from them when I caught a glimpse of movement behind the booths.

It was an old woman carrying a cardboard box, which she heaved up onto the tailgate of her little pickup truck.

I noticed she'd forgotten to secure the box's flaps, which allowed a tiny furry black snout to poke out.

The hippie hawking the soaps kept my girlfriend from moving on to the next booth by making her an offer she couldn't refuse. It was something about an end-of-day two-for-one special, and that allowed me to keep staring at the box, and the snout, which was joined by a little probing black paw.

The old man who painted the scary horses stopped packing up his car to chat up the old woman with the box. He was clearly smitten with her, and she seemed very receptive to his flirting.

If they hadn't been so caught up in their elderly courtship she would have noticed the box was tipping. It rocked one way and canted the other, and then tumbled off the tailgate and popped open when it hit the ground.

And two chubby black puppies rolled out.

The confused pups could have easily run off in another direction, or in opposite directions, but they didn't. They got their disproportionately big feet under them and charged hip-to-hip together in unsure gangly hops right toward the soap booth.

And straight toward me.

They dodged around the leaning stack of scary horse paintings, ducked under the rack of unsold expensive soaps, and then shot out from under the booth's tablecloth right into my crouched waiting arms.

Their wiggling little warm black bodies twisted and spun against me, and then one of them discovered my face and chomped down on my nose with his puppy needle teeth.

The old woman slipped between the booths to apologize. As she smiled down at the three of us she explained she had brought the runt orphan mutt siblings to the fair to get them adopted.

She also said it had been overcast and a little chilly all day, so the fair had been slow and everyone was packing up early. The pups had napped cuddled up together on their blanket in the box behind her craft honey display all day without so much as a peep from them or one person noticing her scribbled puppy adoption sign.

I turned from the old woman to my girlfriend, whose scowl had been replaced by a smirk.

Her smirk curled up into a full smile, and she nodded at the expectant ask on my beaming face.

And then she nodded again to agree with my silent assertion that it would be a damn crime to separate them.

She was clutching that children's book to her chest, so in a flash of inspired brilliance I suggested we name our new pups Spot and Smudge.

We ended up saying those names a thousand times that spring, sometimes yelling them, and sometimes patiently hissing them between gritted teeth as we wiped their muddy paws and took things they shouldn't have out of their mouths and cleaned up their accidents. We grumbled their names after they gnawed little chunks out of the chair legs, and when they exploded with tandem midnight barks for no reason, and in response to their alternating sneaky gas attacks as we held our noses.

But we also proudly introduced them to people who paused to coo at their cuteness, and fake-admonished them for slobbering on us during the jowl-flopping car rides, where they sat on our laps and hung their heads out the windows. We cheered their wrestling as they chased each other through the waves at the beach, and endlessly praised them for trying so very hard to please us. But mostly we wheezed their names doubled over with laughter at just about everything they did as they quickly grew big and strong and smart and handsome.

I had many fun Saturdays at work with my pair of perfectly behaved dogs, who became the office mascots and learned to make the rounds to politely beg for snacks. And we enjoyed scores of Sundays snuggled up on the couch with our 70-pound feet-warmers, where we received the best tender cheek-kisses and gentle hand-nudges for attention. For several awesome years they bookended us with their wonderful leaning bulks, and stared up at us with those huge brown eyes filled with that special kind of unconditional love.

And then we had the terrible rollercoaster of Smudge's cancer, and the heartbreak of watching his depressed sibling mope around the house for months after he was gone.

But then my wife and I got to see Spot's tail spin around in excited circles when he welcomed our two girls.

He critiqued our rookie diaper changing with his skeptical peaked brows, and very gently licked away their infrequent tears, and kept their whispered giggled secrets, and guarded their blanket forts, and ate their sneaked-under-the-table vegetables, and sat on the couch with them with his gangly legs hanging over like a human's.

I am convinced he hung around into his teen years, and theirs, just to make sure we were all going to be fine.

Which we are.

Our girls have grown into accomplished happy young women, and I ended up writing several novels about Spot and Smudge, which has allowed me to retire early to spoil our first grandchild.

I'm just waiting for him to get old enough so I can gift him a pair of adopted rescue black mutt siblings.

And before he picks out names for his new pups I'm going to tell him a story about having to work on the weekend, and arguing with Grandma about it, and stopping for an impulse donut, and getting stuck in line behind that chatty couple who rambled on about their cute Saturday plans.

Promises Kept and Broken

– Ann Herlihy Jaroncyk –

I had made a promise never to have another dog. It wasn't that I didn't love them. Oh, no, just the opposite. I had been rescuing dogs in need all my life, one after another, as did my mother before me. I was tired of making final decisions for ailing pets and, frankly, saying goodbye.

The promise held until Pal entered my life.

My husband John and I often visited our friend Shirley on nearby Plum Island. She had two large dogs who competed for food. Pal, on the other hand, was small, scrawny, pitiful, and, for the most part, ignored. He never barked, didn't complain; he was like Lazarus the biblical beggar who sat among the well-fed and begged for scraps. John was crazy about this little Papillion. He would stash several dog biscuits in his pocket and give one to each of the big dogs, saving the rest for Pal. I watched as my stoic husband fell in love. I was happy to have John enjoy his friend as long as the little dog maintained his permanent address at Shirley's.

Fate stepped in. Shirley developed brain cancer. She kept this secret until a few weeks before she died. The loss blindsided family and friends. Plans were made for her final resting place, closing the home, and disposing of years of belongings. Family and friends gathered at Shirley's to eat, drink, and say goodbye.

Shirley was a free spirit. Her ashes would be scattered into her beloved Atlantic Ocean. A skiff was built to hold her ashes, which would be towed behind a small motorboat and scattered at sea. Three friends anchored the boats while the remaining mourners watched from her balcony while drinking champagne. We would know when the ashes reached the sea when we saw the skiff light up in flames. Little did we know the Coast Guard would not look favorably on the final plan.

Afterward, John and I sat in our favorite spots at Shirley's house, looking around where we spent many happy hours. I asked, "What plans does the family have to find homes for the dogs?" Silence. The two big dogs were already placed, but sad little Pal had nowhere to go. The family was thinking they might have to put him down.

I spoke before my brain kicked in. "We will take him." John held onto his chair, and a huge smile crossed his face.

Pal needed to leave Shirley's home sooner rather than later. Kmart opened at 8 a.m. I was there when the store opened. I bought a leash, dog dishes, and food and rushed to Shirley's. At 9 o'clock, I placed the leash on Pal and brought him to our place, his new home. Pal immediately sat at John's feet. I could feed and walk him, but Pal had a new best friend. I had been replaced.

John loved Pal. Pal reciprocated. Then John's mesothelioma, contracted in Southeast Asia in the '60s, escalated, and he was dependent on oxygen. Pal knew he had a job. He carefully watched as home health aides, nurses, and EMTs cycled in and out of our house. Months passed. John's health deteriorated, and he entered a hospice facility. My days were spent caring for Pal and spending precious hours with my beloved. Hospice rules allowed crated dogs to visit, and Pal traveled with me.

Then John's last day came. Pal lay in his crate as I held John's hand, listening to his labored breathing. I let Pal out of his carrier. He jumped on the bed and nestled in John's arm, then moved to John's feet; I held John's hand as he took his last breath. I lifted Pal, put him in his crate, and, in tears, waited for help.

Pal lived one more year. He lay by my side of the bed and brought me comfort. Finally, his little body gave up. I had him cremated. He was John's Pal, so I sneaked his urn into the cemetery. While no one was looking, I dug a hole above John's coffin. I said a prayer and buried the urn. Now, they are together again.

I promised again that I would never get another pet, as I was heartbroken over losing my husband and then Pal. The condo John and I had moved to didn't easily accommodate a dog. A few months later, I broke my promise and found myself at a cat rescue shelter. I couldn't stay away. The most adoptable cats were in the front of the shelter. The older ones, harder to place, were in a back room.

"Can I see the other cats?" I asked. I found a mangy cat hugging the back wall. I was warned that the cat often refused his litter box, the reason he had been brought to the shelter. No one wanted him. He would not greet any visitor, at least that is what I was told. His name was Vern.

I knew he had to be mine.

I renamed him Curious George, known as CG. CG was with me for several years. When he became seriously ill, I again had to make the final decision to let a loved pet go. My heart was broken. It was during the Covid-19 outbreak, so I couldn't hold him while he passed away. I came home, tossed everything away, and promised, again, no pets.

I have spent two years without a pet. So far I have held on to my no-pet decision. I fill my need for animal companionship by helping pet owners with their pets, stopping by to feed them and keep them company, and moving in when the owners go on vacation. I call this "getting my dog."

Will I get another pet? My history causes me to doubt if I can resist. I am the oldest of eight children, a caretaker of both children and dogs and a second-generation rescuer. What are the odds?

I still struggle with the decision, but for now am holding onto this promise.

Emotional Support Dog

– Mariana Stone –

It's 5 a.m. I am fast asleep: the kind of deep sleep where I'm not even dreaming. Life is good. I am getting some much-needed rest. But as I fall back into my blissful slumber, I hear a whine. It's soft but quite high-pitched. I am all too familiar with this sound. I hear it again, a little louder. Then again. I am far too sleepy and comfortable to get out of bed to quell this increasingly loud noise. I fall back asleep for what feels like 20 seconds. Whine. This time I am awakened by a significantly louder sound coupled with something jumping toward my face; it's my dog, Izzy, and it's time for me to feed her.

My sweet dog Izzy, a 15-pound West Highland White Terrier, arrived several weeks before I graduated from college. I picked her up from a farm in rural Pennsylvania and sneaked her into my dorm room. She was roughly the size of a guinea pig. She didn't bark. Her fur was soft and she loved to chew. We made it through two weeks un-detected before I moved back home to Maine and settled into a new life post-college.

Her personality fits the mold of a typical Westie; she is rambunctious, curious, and in tune with the wildlife in my backyard. As my companion, Izzy and I have been through many moves, a degree (or two), a husband, and the birth of my daughter. My favorite part of Izzy is that she loves me unreservedly and has been my rock through many difficult times. What is it about unconditional love that makes it so challenging for humans, though in dogs, love is without question and never changes? I've learned that dogs can have complex emotions.

When I was in labor with my daughter, Izzy was glued to my side, refusing to go outside to go to the bathroom. She saw that I was in pain and needed comfort. I left abruptly to go to the hospital and when I came back Izzy seemed like she was upset with me, avoiding me for several days. She finally came around, but the experience gave me some insight into the different thoughts and emotions dogs can experience. Izzy is always a solid in my life; whether I am tripping over her because she is under my feet, or if I am feeling emotional and she picks up on it, she is truly an affectionate and wonderful dog.

In 2020, several months after the birth of my daughter, I had a postpartum depression episode and ended up at a local hospital. I was juggling a new baby and full-time work.

In addition, I had just found out that I had been abused by a close relative. It shocked me to my core. I was not sleeping well and was constantly tired. One night I was so anxious my body felt like it could not settle down. I had many tools that I was aware could help with anxiety and so I used them – first exercising, then taking a hot bath. Finally, whenever I tried to sleep it felt too scary and that I was afraid of the dark.

I felt like a child, worried about what lurks when there is no light. Even into comparing it to emptiness and death. I started to realize that my mind was not well, so I called 911. I was taken to the hospital. I spent a week on the unit, experiencing a different kind of life than previously. I had very few obligations. Meals were made for me. In some ways, it almost felt like a vacation.

But being hospitalized was the most difficult time in my life. I missed my family terribly. I was unable to see my daughter for one long week – I had to fight the nurses to allow me to pump breast milk. I was quite nervous in the new environment.

After that, I was discharged and completed a partial hospitalization program where I learned more about trauma and abuse. I had struggled and found myself depressed at times and unsure how to cope. The program taught me how to mitigate and process emotions during difficult times. Depression does not simply disappear once you have been discharged from the hospital. It takes time and skills and is quite often a lifelong challenge. Eventually, through a lot of hard work, I was able to cope with what happened.

One day, when I was feeling sad, my mother said to me, "When you feel down, squeeze Izzy and I promise it will help." I thought about it, but then quickly forgot. Several days later I was feeling down and I remembered what my mother told me. I got into bed and pulled Izzy in close. She gave me an appreciative lick. She was so soft and snuggly. I could feel my mood shifting instantly and I was better. She was alert to my emotions and she could tell I needed a lick to improve my mood. Additionally, she stayed by me, steadfast in her devotion to me without question.

I continue this ritual quite often, even though the depression has improved dramatically. It feels good to hold Izzy close. She improved my mood many times. Though she often wakes me up with a raucous noise, after she is fed, she comes into my bed and snuggles with me. It is one of the best feelings and I constantly feel very loved. Izzy is 12 now, and though I do sometimes feel down or anxious, I look down and Izzy is right by my side, completely in tune with my emotions, and for that I am grateful.

No Permanent Name

– June Hunter –

It was quiet on the road after the little dog disappeared. I was sad the poor thing was gone and hoped nothing bad had happened to it but delighted the yapping had stopped. I knew they thought I took it, but they never should have gone away and left it behind with only the live-in housekeeper to care for it. I figured she'd had enough of its constant yapping as well and banished the dog.

I saw the dog on the street a few days before it disappeared. It must have escaped through the bars on the gate; it was jumping around in the middle of the road, barking at nothing. Its white coat was matted, its nose pink, and its weepy eyes didn't look too healthy either. I was reluctant to pick it up in case it snapped at me, but I did anyway, and it was so light that it felt as though I was picking up a live chicken. It licked my hand and then laid its head on my arm.. I held it closer and scratched its skinny neck as I carried it back to the housekeeper.

"Sorry, ma'am," she said. "He doesn't want to stay inside."

My neighbors are lovely people, don't get me wrong. Andrew is a passive soul and Jenny keeps to herself most of the time. I don't understand why they got their Maltese/Poodle since they seemed unable to offer any attention to the little dog. I blame that lack of attention for turning their pet into a neurotic yapper. It yelped at the trees during the day and at the stars at night, but the strange thing was the owners didn't seem to notice..

"What's his name?" I asked Jenny one day as I passed their gate. She could hardly hear me above the barking and was concentrating on trying to keep her foot across the dog's chest to stop him from escaping through the bars. "Name?" she said. "We haven't given him a permanent name yet. We're waiting to see what sort of name he becomes."

Maybe *Yappee*, I thought.

I got their phone number on the pretext that good neighbors always exchange phone numbers in case of an emergency. Then, I phoned them in the middle of the night. I was awake at 3 in the morning because of their dog! I could hear it beyond the road, and on the other end of the telephone line when Andrew answered the phone.

"Do you not hear him?" I asked.

"Not really," said groggy Andrew. "But I'll bring him inside."

For me, it was hard to work with all that barking. Waiting for it to stop. Feeling brief relaxation flowing along my nerves when it did. Only for it to start up again as soon as I began to work, and my peace was, once again, shattered. My stomach muscles contracted, my jaw clenched, my nails dug into my palms, and when I closed my eyes, I could see red mist swirling around inside my head.

At least I wasn't living right next door to them, and I wondered what Karen and Luigi thought. Karen works from home too. She's a graphic designer. I'm not sure what Luigi does. He makes great pizzas though. One of the first things he did when they moved in was to build a pizza oven in the garden, and we were lucky enough to be invited over to sample how well it worked. That was before Andrew and Jenny moved in next door to them.

"I've heard that if you get them neutered it helps," Karen said. "Or take them for social visits to other dogs."

But poor little Yappee never went on visits, or even walks for that matter. Now he had disappeared and the only thing the housekeeper could tell Andrew and Jenny when they got back from their holiday was that she noticed a car pull up on the other side of the street. A woman with longish brown hair, just like mine, got out and took him away.

"Do you know what happened to our dog?" Andrew asked me in his quiet, non-confrontational voice.

"No idea, Andrew," I said.

"Our housekeeper said she saw a woman take him away."

"Well, it wasn't me. Sorry, but I don't know what happened to him."

But I did have a vague idea of what might have taken place, as Karen and I had been discussing a possibility the day before.

"I bet you it's a woman who lives in the next block," said Karen. "She's been known to kidnap people's pets."

"I know who you mean. I heard that she "borrowed' the dog and took him to the vet to have him neutered."

"That's the one," said Karen. "She did the same thing to the tortoiseshell cat from up the road. Claimed it was impregnating too many females in the neighborhood and there were too many kittens looking for homes."

"I wonder if Andrew knows about her," I said. "Do you think we should tell him?"

Karen looked off into the distance, and we both listened to the silence around us.

I'm not sure if anyone ever mentioned the neighbor and her antics to Jenny and Andrew, but they found out about her soon enough. She turned up at their gate clutching a white, recently groomed Maltese/Poodle under her arm. I watched them from my open study window and could just about hear their conversation.

"I took your pooch," she said as the little dog squirmed in excitement to see his owners again.

"Why?" I heard Andrew ask. "What right did you have?" I could tell he was trying to sound aggrieved, but his voice was like a whine.

"The right of a concerned animal lover," she said. "He was in a dreadful state. You've never even brushed his coat."

I could see Karen leaning out of her study window. She looked across at me and waved.

"I've had him neutered as well," said the woman. "And there are some drops for his eyes, and the vet's bill. I expect to be compensated for it all."

"Indeed!" said Andrew.

Jenny lifted the little dog out of the woman's arms and held him close to her as she kissed the top of his head.

"Thank you," she said. "We just never got around to doing all that."

"What's his name, anyway?"

"I think we'll call him Yippee," said Jenny. "Yip for short."

"Just to show how happy we are to have him back," said Andrew.

Yip licked Jenny's face and when she put him down, he followed her into the house, tail wagging, yapping his joy at being home.

Maggie, Undaunted

– Kathleen J. Mackin –

It was 1979, and I had just finished a master's degree at the University of Georgia and was staying on in Athens to teach in the public school system. I was hunting for an apartment and happened instead to find a small, appealing two-bedroom house for rent on the outskirts of town. I rented the house and moved in, but soon realized I was not sleeping well and was feeling uncomfortable.

A friend of mine suggested that I get a dog. A dog? I wasn't sure I wanted to be tied down with a dog as I only planned to stay in Georgia another year or so and didn't know exactly where I would go next. But he insisted we go out to the Georgia animal shelter and just look around at the dogs they had to offer.

The "animal shelter" itself was a shock. You really couldn't call it a shelter, but it was basically a large fenced area managed by prison inmates. There was a collection of small to medium-sized unhappy mutts milling around, barking, and fighting. Amid this chaos, one dog stood out, a large – seemingly full-grown – female Collie/Shepherd mix with a golden face and a black and ginger coat.

She was sitting in the middle of the mayhem, looking around

as if to say, "Well, it's not the Ritz, but it'll do." I thought to myself, if that dog can be calm and happy here, then I can certainly make a comfortable home for her, even though I knew little about caring for a dog.

The inmate caretakers more or less begged me to take a puppy, but I wanted a guard dog, not a puppy I would need to train. They told me the dog I chose hadn't been surrendered to the shelter but was found wandering on the highway. After they gave up suggesting puppies to me, the caretakers reluctantly released the Collie Shepherd into my care. My friend and I opened the back door of my car, and she hopped in, positioned herself squarely in the middle of the back seat, and waited calmly for her next adventure to begin. No questions asked.

For the next 14 years of her adventuresome life, the middle of the back seat was the regal position she always held when riding in the car. Friends who found themselves driving behind me in traffic in our small town would comment that from the back window of my car, it looked as if I was chauffeuring the Queen of England wearing a fur coat. They fully expected her to be sporting pearls and carrying a handbag as she emerged from the car.

Once we got back to town, I immediately took her to a vet to have her checked out, cleaned up, and vaccinated. The vet believed she was at least a year old and in reasonably good condition except for skin and fur issues that would clear up with treatment. I brought her home, fed her, and named her Maggie; before sunset, I had fallen in love.

Maggie was every bit the guard dog I had hoped for. Her size and bark were enough to provide a warning, but true to her collie nature, she was also a love who drew people to her immediately. And she was a dog fully in charge of her own destiny.

Within months of Maggie's arrival at my home, I held a Halloween party. I was totally distracted with guests and preparations, but several friends who arrived told me Maggie was in the next yard mating with the red Siberian Husky who lived there. I thought nothing of it, as I was told by the inmate caretakers that Maggie was spayed. But within a month, Maggie was displaying a wide girth, and after two months, she delivered nine puppies. They were all beautiful, furry red Husky and Collie/Shepherd mixes – four females and five males. Two friends and I attended the birth of the puppies with champagne at the ready, but Maggie did all the work.

The births took more than 11 hours. We started naming the puppies as they emerged: Uno, Dos, Tres, Quatro, and Cinco. As the champagne took hold, we switched to real names like Pancho, Pablo, and Pedro. And for some reason, the last puppy was named Kit. While I fretted over Maggie, who was feeding and caring for nine healthy puppies, she took it in stride, rarely showing impatience; she was a wonderfully patient mother.

At about eight weeks, the puppies were ready to find new homes. I knew this would be challenging, but I engaged Maggie. I took four of them to the school where I was teaching to show them to the kindergarten class. Before I left, three of them were claimed by teachers. My neighbor, who owned the daddy, a red Husky, took another one. Two came with Maggie and me to the farmers market and found homes. A friend took the seventh puppy and a professor at the university took the eighth. Sensing a special bond between Maggie and her furry blonde and strawberry red puppy, Kit, I decided to keep her. In truth, Maggie decided to keep her. They were inseparable and Kit was a real "mini-me." We were now a family of three.

We eventually left Athens and I took a job in Washington, DC. After a year it became clear that keeping two large dogs in the city was untenable. While it was painful, the three of us "talked" and decided that playful Kit really needed a yard and a loving family with kids. I put an ad in the Washington Post classifieds and wrote the ad from Kit's perspective: "My name is Kit. I'm a lively Shepherd/Husky mix who would love a big yard and some fun kids to play with." Soon after the ad appeared, a 7-year-old boy read it and begged his parents to come see Kit.

The next day, the little boy, his parents, and his three sisters – all redheads, just like Kit – arrived at our place and loved Kit the minute they saw her. Kit had her perfect family, complete with a large house and a sprawling yard in McLean, Va. Maggie and I were blue for a while, and we visited Kit's new family several times to comfort ourselves. The little boy beamed with pride over his new dog and told us she slept every night with the family's pet bunny.

Maggie was always intrepid, full of life, finding adventure in every new place we lived. When she was 13, we moved to Rye, N.H., where Maggie, at her advanced age, seemed to come alive, relishing the ocean air and walking on the beach. Sadly, just two short years after our move, Maggie died. I was inconsolable.

When the vet gave me her ashes, he told me that they discovered a BB lodged in her body. I thought back to what the inmate at the shelter in Georgia told me–that she was found wandering on the highway. I believe she was running away from a bad situation, taking destiny into her own hands. She saved her own life and in the process found her way to me and enriched my life beyond measure.

Poolside Code Blue

– Deborah D'Avolio –

It was a beautiful summer Sunday afternoon and my day off from working a 12-hour weekend shift as a registered nurse in a Level 1 trauma center. Usually, the backyard was filled with loud music, splashing in the pool, or kids playing basketball. But this day it was just my husband, Len, and me. It was a trifecta: beautiful weather, a day off, and our teenagers out for the day.

Our 9-month-old Lab looked a bit puzzled by the absence of youthful playmates. Where were they? When the teens were hanging at our pool, she was ecstatic because they never tired of playing with her. She would run chasing the ball they threw endlessly. Sometimes Zoe ran until her paw pads would bleed from charging up and down the concrete pool deck. When the kids were there, their energy matched the pup's. But not this Sunday.

We relaxed, grabbed our floats, coffee, and the Sunday paper. As we floated in the pool, we saw Zoe sitting in the garden lazing in the sun. "This is so relaxing," my husband said.

While I was engrossed in the newspaper, Len suddenly yelled, "Deb, Zoe just ate a bee!"

Was he sure? Yes.

"I saw her watching the bee and then opening her mouth and swallowing it." I jumped out of the pool to check on her. Zoe toppled over and collapsed. White froth began coming out of her mouth, her eyes rolled back. Her gums were pale instead of the normal color, which meant oxygen deprivation. Very quickly it dawned on me, this was something I had seen and treated many times. Zoe was in anaphylactic shock.

Several thoughts simultaneously ran through my mind. I needed immediate resources: an IV, Epi Injection, Benadryl, oxygen, and Solumedrol. But I was in my yard, in a bathing suit, not in the Emergency Department. We needed a vet with emergency services on a Sunday afternoon. I shouted to Len.

"There isn't enough time to travel to Boston! Find an emergency vet near here. Zoe won't make it downtown."

I knew she was dying in my arms. Our girl was unresponsive, still frothing at the mouth with labored breathing.

Think, think, think. Oh yes, it came to me. Because of my own seafood allergy, I always have remedies stored in our medicine cabinet. While my husband was searching for a vet, I ran into my medicine cabinet and grabbed my Epi-pen and Benadryl. I was frightened because although I knew how to treat people, I didn't know how to treat dogs. However, I had no choice but to try. I opened the epinephrine and injected it into her skin on the base of her neck as I have seen the vet do for Zoe's routine immunizations.

Within a few minutes after the injection, Zoe opened her eyes, but I could see she was still in distress. As she became responsive, I opened the bottle of Benadryl and poured some into her mouth. Thankfully, she swallowed it.

My husband found an emergency vet in the next town and let the office know we were on our way.

"OK, let's go, we have to get there before she dies."

Len opened the car door and placed Zoe on my lap. Off we

went, Len and I in our bathing suits on our way to the vet's office. I watched the speedometer move quickly and we were exceeding the limit. Zoe lay quietly panting on my lap. In what seemed like forever, we got to the vet's office. Len carried Zoe as we both ran bursting through the doorway. The waiting room was full of people. As we ran in, I shouted to folks in the waiting room.

"This is a life-threatening emergency, the vet is going to be busy."

We ran down a long corridor and found the vet. Zoe was in distress. I gave the report as I would in the emergency department.

"Nine-month-old female Lab, in anaphylactic shock from swallowing a bee. I gave her Epi and Benadryl. She has come around a bit but is still in shock. We need an IV stat."

He looked at me incredulously. He set up an IV bag of fluid and attempted to start the IV but could not get a vein. People in shock have vascular collapse and starting an IV can be very challenging. I watched him try several times. I was becoming alarmed that he couldn't get a vein. I pleaded with him to let me try because she was dying.

He moved aside and I got the IV in and started the fluids. Epinephrine, Benadryl, and Solumedrol were pushed into the IV line and Zoe began to respond. Within 20 minutes she was back to normal.

Once the vet and I were out of emergency mode, I began to feel the impact of what had happened.

I started to shake realizing how close we came to losing Zoe. Our entire family would have been devastated. I turned to the vet and asked him if he was going to admit her to the animal hospital.

"Hell no, you are taking her home with you. I have never treated a dog in anaphylactic shock. This is a first for me. You do what you need to do for her."

He explained that pets in shock usually die at home before they ever get to emergency vet care.

"Deb, let's get Zoe home," Len said grinning.

Something profound happened to Zoe after the bee incident.

She changed from a puppy to a mature dog and became attentive to all of us. If one of us was upset or having a bad day, she sensed it and would stay close. As a family, we were so thankful that Zoe recovered. The children nicknamed her Zoe the Zen Dog for consistently giving us peace, love, and happiness from that day on.

Dad Said No Dogs

– Rebecca Mayer –

For as long as I can remember, I have been in love with horses. I played with toy horses instead of dolls and built a swinging wooden horse to ride on in the basement. Although we lived in rural Vermont, we did not have land enough for a horse and did not live near a horse farm. Once I had a friend who owned a pony, but that friendship ended when she realized that I was really only interested in the pony.

Finally, after years of disappointment, I decided, at age 10, to settle for a dog. This too presented a possibly insurmountable problem, as my father's decisive response was a firm "No!" Not to be denied, I armed myself with arguments to counter his expressed reasons for denying me, only to be taken aback by his rejections of what I thought were very convincing points.

Seeking support and insight into this surprising development, I entreated my mother to support my cause. To my surprise, she was on my dad's side! This puzzled me, as she was an animal lover and a naturalist from a family that had owned many animals. I'd assumed that getting a dog, just a dog, mind you, would be a done deal.

After all, Grampa had three dogs, a couple of cats, a cow, chickens, a sheep, a goat, white rats, a hog, and a monkey. We'd already owned – cats, snakes, tree frogs, rabbits, and Monarch butterflies. Granted the rabbits caused problems when two rabbits became 250, but I was only asking for one measly dog. Since I couldn't have a horse, this seemed reasonable to me.

Mom clarified the problem by telling me about the Collie dog my dad had lost to old age when he was a boy – a loss so painful for him that he could not bear the thought of owning and losing another dog. My reaction to his reason for not having another dog was to decide that it made having a dog even more important. I immediately set out to find a way around this roadblock.

It wasn't long before an opportunity presented itself. A local grocery store advertised a "Doggie in the Window" contest. The prize was a purebred Cocker Spaniel puppy. All you had to do to enter was to name the puppy. Perfect! The red fur on the puppy shown on the poster made me think of a chipmunk.

"Hah," I thought. "I'll call the puppy Chippy."

I hurried in to get the entry forms and, whoops, Dad said "No" again! This time Mom stepped in and argued him out of it by pointing out that there wasn't much chance of my winning. I, of course, knew better. Several months later, Chippy arrived and my life with dogs began.

By this time, I had read many dog books and really wanted a standard Collie, a German Shepherd, or a Doberman. That meant: A big dog that could do heroic things. However, Chippy, or Robin's Red Man, his registered name, was exactly the right dog for me. He was beautiful, with a silky, wavy, red-gold coat, beseeching amber eyes, and soft floppy ears that flew back against his head as he ran. He learned quickly and was endlessly forgiving. Small enough to travel with us in the family car, he accompanied us on most trips. As he feared he would, my father fell in love with Chippy, as did everyone else in my family.

Soon after his arrival, Chippy began teaching me what was required of a dog owner. The primary characteristic was patience, a trait in which I was sadly deficient. This didn't bother Chippy, but it bothered me a lot because I knew I was being unfair to him. I wanted him to be the best-trained dog ever. He wanted to be the happiest dog ever. He eventually learned what I wanted to teach him after I learned to introduce behavior in small steps with ample rewards. One pleasure of owning a dog is their innate desire to be with and please their humans. Chippy and I became inseparable.

We did, however, have points of serious disagreement. Chippy was determined to find and eat toads. Somehow, in those days, there seemed to be toads everywhere. He found them and, before he could be stopped, he seized them and suffered the consequences of their poisons. He would froth at the mouth, vomit and generally be very sick, while we tried to wash the poison out of his mouth and reproved him for, once again, disobeying our instructions to "Leave Toads Alone!"

On approaching anything else, he obeyed the order to "Leave it!" but toads were too tempting for him. Try as we might, we never succeeded in changing this behavior. His other main failing was his desire to chase the milk truck. All other vehicles were safe from his attacks, but he ignored all orders to cease and desist from his pursuit of the milk truck. Eventually one day he was hit by a truck. He was bruised and not otherwise injured or even deterred by this encounter, but we foresaw a future disaster if his behavior continued unchecked. We started putting a long leash on him when he was out alone; it seemed like the only way to manage his obsession.

Early in his life, Chippy and our family faced a serious medical crisis; Chippy developed a large cyst under his neck. The cyst was drained several times but always returned. We were told that, when he passed through the gill stage of development in his mother's womb, the gills never completely went away. Chippy would require a delicate, often unsuccessful, surgery to remove all trace of gill tissue, or he would never be well.

While I did not doubt that he would have the surgery and that he would get well – I could accept no other outcome – my parents were seriously concerned by the amount of money involved. Only one surgeon in the area, located in another state, could be found to attempt the surgery and the cost was prohibitive. I was devastated. My lovely parents, to whom I am eternally grateful, borrowed the money for the operation. Luckily for all, the surgery was a success and Chippy went on to live a long and happy life.

When I left Chippy and went off to college, Chippy became my sister's dog. Sure, I returned home, but having met my future husband on the first day of college, my interest in relationships moved from dog to man. Whenever I was home, I was less attentive to Chippy and I spent less and less time at home. Then, at the end of my sophomore year, I married and was gone for good.

I feel sad when I think of how completely I abandoned Chippy, and yet I think that he quite easily transferred his allegiance from me to my sister. I know she loved him too but then she also left for college and Chippy became my parents' dog. I'll always wonder if I betrayed his love and trust. What did he actually think or feel?

Given the intensely close relationships I had with my Border Collies later in life, I imagine that Chippy formed the same kind of attachment.

Kealie: A Black Dog Rescued

– Andrea Stoehr –

Her name was Lily when we met her. She had a smooth black coat, and white toes on her back paws, and she was missing her tail. Her name didn't suit her, but I didn't want to change the sound too much and confuse her, so I thought of Billie for the singer Billie Holiday. However, our 13-year-old daughter, Olivia, insisted she was Kealie. So, Kealie it was. We chose her from the litter in part because we'd heard black dogs were the hardest to place and also because she was the biggest of the rescue dogs available. We hoped that meant she had the most developed bladder and would be the easiest to train. (Spoiler alert: Not true!)

She smiled all the way home and when we let her loose in our field, she ran with her ears flopping up and down like a little girl in pigtails. She repeatedly stumbled over her long legs as she zigzagged across the grass. She came back and squashed her head on my lap – her version of a hug – smelling of grasses and flowers.

We soon learned that Kealie was a chewer. She found a bunch of old broccoli in the compost pile, pulled it out, and ran around as if she had a new chew toy. Her chewing wasn't so funny when she uprooted the Copper Kettle hibiscus plant five times or when she chewed the small Dogwood tree down to a stick in the ground. She may have thought, "DOGwood? It must be for me."

Soon after we rescued Kealie, we took a trip to Martha's Vineyard and brought Kealie along with us. I looked back at one point on our trip to see Olivia painting the dog's nails with green nail polish. Kealie was a great little traveler, and when we rode the bus on the Vineyard, while Dad worked, she'd hop on and fall asleep in the aisle between stops. Martha's Vineyard has a famous restaurant called The Black Dog which sells thousands of T-shirts with a picture of a black dog, so Kealie saw images of herself everywhere, minus the green nail polish of course.

When I think of words to describe Kealie, I think "resourceful." We live in the country, and we had five roosters the year after we brought Kealie home. The birds were notably raucous and noisy, which annoyed her mightily. One day Kealie took it as her job to reprimand one of them for fighting. She grabbed the offending bird by the butt and swam it around the pond in her mouth to teach it a lesson. When she came ashore and let it go, the rooster stumbled up to the rest of the chickens uninjured, properly chastened, and perhaps with an important life lesson learned.

Kealie is also a dog with a large vocabulary. She looks deeply into my eyes when I talk to her and knows quite a few words and commands. I have to be careful about saying WALK, or else I'm nagged into going up the hill for a run. She knows sometimes I need HELP to go feed the chickens. She knows THIRSTY means an after-dinner treat, consisting of a little food and a bowl of water. She understands LATER, BONE, CAR, PEANUT BUTTER, DADDY. Perhaps she will write her autobiography one day.

From the first, Kealie has been terrified of doors. She will not go through one uninvited and doesn't understand that she can nudge the door open from room to room anytime. I worry because if there was a fire, she wouldn't be able to make herself push the door open with her nose to get herself to safety. I'm guessing that her fear of doors dates back to before we adopted her; we learned that she came from a horrific home environment in Kentucky, living in squalid, abusive conditions. We imagine Kealie as a young pup having a door slammed on her as she tried to squeeze through, sadly leaving her with only a nub of a tail to wag.

Now Kealie is 13 and went through a spell of bladder leakage and subsequently had to wear diapers. Fortunately, she recovered when I started walking her more often and her core strengthened. When I broke my foot recently, she understood I had to heal and walked herself around the yard, another indication of just how smart and sensitive she is.

Ever since we discovered a bear in the chicken coop, Kealie has been hesitant to venture out of the yard. All three of us were scared and the bear ran away with corn and feathers stuck to its butt. Our old cat used to bite and scratch, so naturally Kealie was frightened of her as well. Maybe that accounts for her being leery of our new cat Sylvie, although the cat has never attacked or reacted in any way. Resourceful, intelligent, kind-hearted, and just a little bit timid to keep things interesting, that's Kealie!

The Beagle Rescuer

– Donna Ricci –

"Donna, come get your dog. He bit Adelaide," my lifelong friend Yvonne yelled into the phone as she drove her 85-year-old mother-in-law to the ER. I decided this was not the time to remind her that Sammy was not my dog. He was, in fact, her dog. She is the person everyone calls when a Beagle needs a home.

Growing up, Yvonne always wanted a Beagle, but there was no physical or emotional room in the apartment where she, her mother, and brother lived. Every morning, her mother would take the bus to the Orange Line train station for the hour-long trip into Boston, where she worked at Jordan Marsh.

So, when Yvonne married Ron, and they moved to the relative countryside of Connecticut, she got her first beagle, Buster; indeed, the child she and Ron never had. Buster was a yapper, as all beagles are, but his temperament was sweet, and Yvonne basked in the glow of the Norman Rockwell dream she was intent on creating.

The next beagle, Sammy, came along when she received a call from the dog catcher in Everett, Massachusetts, where we grew up. She could not turn away from this courageous beagle playing chicken with an SUV on the Revere Beach Parkway, a few blocks from her childhood home. "He's a bit of a nipper," the dog catcher said in a moment of full disclosure, but Yvonne believed each one just needed love.

Yvonne called Sammy my dog because I was the only one Sammy never bit. I'd like to think it was because, as a psychologist, my empathy connected with the evident puppyhood trauma that resulted in him being alone later in life on a three-lane highway. Yet, while I never implied he should just pull himself up by his paw straps, I suspect he knew I would not accept misbehavior justified based on past traumas.

Zoe, the Savannah southern belle, came next. Yvonne and Ron had moved to the North Shore of Boston, and her mother-in-law moved in after the death of Ron's father. When Yvonne and Ron arrived home from Georgia with Beagle in tow, they asked me, the other trusted female pack leader, to introduce Zoe into the fold. Three Beagles never made for a quiet household, but they eventually blended in a canine version of "My Three Sons."

My own adventures and misadventures in the canine world involved Irish Setters and a mutt named Daisy. While he was in high school, my older brother brought the Irish Setter, Brandy, into the family home. Brandy was a wild one, constantly making a beeline for the street whenever a door was opened. Yvonne had an old clunker of a car, and on more than one occasion, we would cruise the streets to track Brandy down.

The only thing Brandy loved more than a wild jaunt through the neighborhood was a cruise in the car. "Come on, Brandy, let's go for a ride," I would call out when we spotted him bounding down Broadway in Everett. He would leap into the back seat with evident joy for this next adventure. However, a drive around the block was not considered a legitimate ride. It would take at least a 3-mile trip before he would agree to get out of the car and enter the house.

Years after Brandy was gone, another Irish Setter showed up on my doorstep a few days before Christmas, plopping onto the settee on my front porch, looking up as if to ask, "Where's my martini and slippers?" When I saw the blood coming out of his forehead, I convinced the "Setter that Came for Christmas," as I started to think of him, to get into my car with the tried-and-true call of my childhood. "Hey, let's go for a ride." Just like Brandy, he jumped at the chance. The drive to Angell Memorial Animal Hospital in Boston was about a 15-mile trip; it was one Brandy would have envied. I felt content delivering this holiday surprise into the safe arms of the hospital, knowing they would make sure he was home for Christmas.

This was not the only stray that graced the backseat of my car after some type of trauma. One evening, a friend and I were returning from dinner when we spotted a mutt roaming the street, looking confused. We called the phone number on the tags. The intoxicated man who answered said the dog belonged to his daughter, who was serving overseas in the military. Grudgingly, he gave me his address. When we got there, the man moseyed over to the car and yelled, "Daisy, come on." Daisy was having none of it. She stayed firmly entrenched in my back seat. If truth be told, we had only gone a mile or two, not long enough to be considered a proper ride in the canine world. I suggested it might be better if I kept Daisy for the night and brought her back in the morning when sobriety might prevail. As the man accepted my offer without a backward glance, I understood why she wandered away in the first place.

Who could I call at 9:30 on a Saturday night to get supplies for Daisy's last-minute overnight stay? The Beagle Rescuer. In the 10 minutes it took to get to her house, Yvonne had pulled together everything a dog could need for a day, a week, or a month! Food and bowls to go with it, a leash, a dog bed, a blanket, and flea spray. She gave me detailed instructions on what to do in any situation that might arise.

Daisy jogged up the 52 stairs to my condominium with youthful exuberance, settling into her new bed after a nourishing meal. The next day, when I took Daisy back, the brother of the woman serving our country in the Middle East, was anxiously waiting. Upon seeing him, Daisy bounced out of my car, eager to be with someone who showed he wanted her in his life. Just like all the dogs that had come before, when she was in need, she had no qualms about asking a stranger to take care of her. She received the love with gratitude and then basked in the familiar love waiting for her at home.

I never owned a dog myself, yet being part of the Beagle Pack and unofficial fostering brought contentment. As each Beagle passed, though, Yvonne felt the heaviness of the loss. Saving those with four paws who were alone and neglected gave her purpose. She thrived in their unconditional love, but plummeted when they were gone. Years of those descents took their toll and she could not survive them.

When it came to lessons that our animal friends teach us, she missed the critical point. Every one of those dogs called out to be rescued with a howl or a bite, intuitively knowing they had the right to be saved.

Yvonne never bit. How I wish she had.

Dog Is Our Co-Pilot

– Stacey Newman Weldon –

Poodles are supposed to be smart, while Labradors and Golden Retrievers are known for their generous hearts. What do you get when you mix all three? That would be Brady, our lovable, goofy, ball-chomping Doodle-Doodle, who had more heart than brains. He was exactly what our broken family needed.

Brady came into our lives shortly after I moved into a cottage, separating from my husband. Our two young sons alternated between the homes. We had never owned a dog before because my ex and I never liked the thought of putting our pet in a kennel for vacations or spending time alone for long hours while we were at work. The boys lobbied hard for a dog and finally won.

We drove as a family to get a puppy from a breeder, who was more than three hours away. Because of my allergies, we had to find a hypoallergenic breed, which we couldn't find at the Humane Society or other shelters. Apparently, Brady's dad, a Labradoodle, had "jumped the fence" to see his sweetie, a Goldendoodle. Since this litter wasn't a pure mix, the pups were priced accordingly. It was love at first sight for our little Doodle-Doodle.

Brady's schedule was the same as the boys, spending time at alternating places. He learned that it was OK to be on the couch at one house but not the other, the same thing with beds. He grew into a medium-large dog, weighing about 65 pounds. He outgrew where we were, so I bought a house with a backyard. Who knows how long I would have stayed in that little cottage if it weren't for him! He had a funny way of slinking onto surfaces he wasn't supposed to be on. First, he would put his head on the couch (or bed), then a paw, then an elbow as he slowly leaned more of his body forward. Inch by inch, he managed to get his body onto the couch and snuggle. Those big brown eyes showed that all he wanted was to be with us.

With two kinds of retrievers in his genetics, you would think he'd be great at playing catch. Nope. He loved playing with the ball, not retrieving it and giving it back. Tug of war with a ball in his mouth was his idea of fun. We had baskets of old tennis balls for him. He often tried to have more than one or two in his mouth, making us laugh endlessly when he tried to get that third or fourth one in! Sometimes he seemed to treat tennis balls like chewing gum. One time, we were throwing the ball in the house, and he slid across the kitchen floor, crashing into the fridge. I think the dent is still there.

He loved playing in the snow. Brady was annoying when it came time to shovel the driveway; every shovelful was nothing but snowballs that he had to play with and devour. With his Poodle hair, there were many times he'd come in with snow stuck to him everywhere. He stood patiently inside when we picked off all those bits of snow. Eventually, he had his towel by the back door, and he learned that getting wet or snowy resulted in a glorious body rub!

If the boys went on vacation with their dad, Brady either went with them or stayed with me, and vice versa, for my holidays with the kids. Not once was he put in a kennel. One time I drove with him to visit my mom. He sat in the passenger seat, alert to all the cars on the highway. I looked over and knew that this dog was my co-pilot.

Each of us in the family had a special connection with Brady, and he loved us all unconditionally. He was there when we needed someone to hug and talk through our problems. While my ex and I disagreed on many things, we never disagreed over Brady. That dog's heart was so big; his overflowing love helped us become a new form of family in a way I never expected.

Years later, the young boys have become men, and my ex and I developed a friendship that involved Brady still sharing households. Brady, in his last years, started having seizures and was misdiagnosed with epilepsy. His final seizure was at my ex's home, and I rushed over when called. My ex and I drove together, in the same minivan we had picked him up in as a baby, to the emergency vet hospital. It was there we learned he had a brain tumor and wouldn't survive. We called the boys so that they could say their goodbyes over the phone.

As I leaned in to hold and kiss him one last time, I swear I heard him say, "It's OK, Mama." My sons called me mom. But I knew that Brady would call me Mama. It was his way of letting me know he was going over the rainbow bridge and his heart would still be with us. All these years later, I feel his spirit bouncing along beside me when I'm walking places he would have enjoyed or when I find a random tennis ball. Brady had a big, generous heart that will always be the glue of our broken and mended family.

The "God is My Co-Pilot" concept impacts me. I remember thinking that dog is god spelled backward, and the sentiment that God is love and by your side, then it made sense that Brady in the passenger seat was my co-pilot. With his strong spirit still showing up in our lives, watching over us, and sending his love, I believe Brady is just that.

Otis, the Caring Canine

– Jen Piliero –

Otis the Goldendoodle was an unofficial therapy dog long before he and I began volunteering at Caring Canines. He was a source of entertainment, comfort, and companionship for everyone in the household. Many couldn't imagine our pup had the focus or calm temperament required. He was goofy, had excitable energy, made people laugh with his antics, and could hop like a kangaroo.

"Not exactly therapy dog material," some would say, shaking their heads.

Well, as was often the case, Otis surprised his family. He and I worked together, and in 2015, he passed his test and became a delightful visitor in many facilities and communities. A few visits will forever stand out.

One of those visits was to a local hospital. Otis and I were doing room-to-room visits on the pediatric floor. As with all visits, patients consent to a visit with a therapy dog, and a staff member always accompanies us. On this particular day, Otis and I visited with several young patients who spoke of their pups at home and how much they missed them. Seeing another dog, even though not theirs, helped lift their spirits.

Otis and I entered a room where a young boy was in bed, his dad by his side. The father quietly told us that his son was nauseous, had had a tough morning, and most likely would not be up for a visit. We were about to leave the room when the boy motioned for us to come over. His father stepped aside, and Otis gently approached the bedside.

The boy reached his hand over to Otis and began whispering to him. As we stood there, his father and a nurse who happened to be in the room noticed his blood pressure steadied, and color returned to this young boy's face. The physical change in this boy was remarkable. We all stood there in silence, witnessing the incredible power of a dog's touch and love, even though moments earlier they had been strangers.

Another visit was to a memory care unit where Otis met up with a reluctant resident. Before this day, she had turned down any and all visits with therapy dogs, not saying anything but consistently waving them off.

I realized the resident was watching Otis and me in a somewhat covert manner as we navigated around the room. I approached her again with Otis and had Otis sit about 5 feet from her. We just stood there. Quietly. Otis locked eyes with her, connecting with his deep brown eyes, his secret language, sharing his love and warmth. She reached out to him, and I had him approach, one cautious step after another, closing the gap between them. She looked away, and then her gaze returned to him. He sat quietly and patiently, somehow knowing that this visit would take time. Within a few minutes, we got even closer. Then Otis got the message that she was ready to pat him. He settled in next to her chair. She motioned that she would prefer him in front of her, so he and I obliged.

I was hesitant and wondered if she would be comfortable being so close to Otis. But he trusted her and knew it was going to be OK. He sat still for what seemed like ages. At one point, she reached over and hugged him, holding him tighter and then rocking back and forth.

Within minutes, I heard her quietly singing to him. Otis, who was always in motion, sat perfectly still and melted into her embrace. She continued singing long after the other residents left the visit and it was wrapping up. I looked up and noticed staff filming the interaction between Otis and this resident.

A staff member leaned in and said that in the years the resident had been at this facility, she had never uttered a word – not one single word. They had never heard her talk, much less sing. I was astonished. Yet, as I watched Otis sit quietly sharing his love, I reflected that this wasn't astonishing at all.

Otis brought his magical healing energy to the job few thought he could do.

Charlie, the Community-Building Cockalier

– Carole Noveck –

Our family lost our adored 13-year-old Vizsla to cancer in the summer of 2011. Because a family dog had been and would be so important to us, we realized we couldn't rush into choosing just any dog. Being patient and waiting for the right one to cross our path was the way to proceed.

In March of the following year, for the first time in more than a decade, I was walking alone. Walking dogless is probably better for your health, in terms of physical activity. Maintaining a stride, going where you want to go, without a specific purpose in mind is efficient. People who cross paths may nod, some may smile, or even engage in a few pleasantries. But walking alone is nothing like the adventure of venturing out with an energetic pup. Dogs whose ages are still measured in weeks charge out of the house, sniffing at every tree, barking or whining at some potential competition for attention, pulling toward something potentially edible or, even better, richly fragrant.

On one of my solitary, dogless strolls, a young woman I hadn't seen before came my way walking a small multicolored dog that made me pause. I carried a mental list of canine attributes: long floppy ears, curly hair (less shedding), not too big, not too small, long muzzle (better to smell with), large eyes to gaze lovingly, and a lively wiggle of excitement at seeing another body come close. This sweet young thing ticked all the boxes. Most dog walkers are happy to talk about their charges, whether they own them or not.

I found out this puppy came from a kennel 40 minutes away where they imported American Kennel Club-registered breeds from around the country. I soon was told her dog Ed was a Cockalier. A what? She had to repeat it and explained it was a relatively new addition to the carefully bred cross between two spaniel varieties, Cocker and King Charles. Ed's litter was among the first "Cockaliers" distributed around the country. According to the AKC, recently designed hybrids were not permitted to breed with others of that combination, until at least one full generation has been observed through lifespan. I wish I knew how/who selected that unappealing and non-descriptive title for the darling creature that developed.

I asked the name and location of the kennel and literally raced home to check out the breeder and make a call. Two of the adorable siblings with the unfortunate name were still available. My husband was agreeable and off we went the same afternoon. Of course, we were "just looking."

One hour later, a black and white 8-week-old puppy with all the features I desired came running down a ramp directly into my lap. He visited with my husband, licking every available inch of exposed skin, and then moved on to someone else. He carefully visited every person and then jumped right back into my lap. I named the puppy Charlie immediately, being half King Charles, even before we made the final decision to buy him. As he looked up at me, I knew he had found me, entrapped me, and joined our family.

As soon as we reached home, Charlie began to create his community. Although our young adult son felt we should look for a larger dog, he couldn't deny that this dog had a charismatic personality. As we walked around the neighborhood, we discovered many people we had not previously met, who were attracted to Charlie. Other dog lovers joined the fan club and even some, "not as fond of dogs" people, liked his friendliness, his silence, and his wiggle. Charlie had a magical way of drawing other dogs and people into his circle. He was easily trained and loved sleeping in his own crate. Within a few weeks, we had a doggie club waiting to meet up on every walk.

When we planned our first vacation after Charlie's arrival, we knew we had to include our new pup. We couldn't bear to put him in the freezing cold plane cargo hold alone, so the location needed to be within driving distance. We assumed that as long as we brought his crate, food, leash, and toy, he would be a cheerful companion, adaptable to anywhere we chose. We needed to find a dog-friendly place to stay. We landed in a rental house with a backyard, next door to a family with shy Oliver.

Oliver was slow to warm up to other dogs, the owners explained, but he was the same weight and age as our Charlie, 10 pounds and 18 months. Charlie and Oliver, the next-door neighbor, circled each other, smelled all the necessary body parts, and decided they were simpatico. After a pleasant time together, we separated the dogs so we could start to explore our new environment. Once out on the street, Oskar, an enormous bloodhound easily five times bigger but the same age, came racing toward Charlie, as far as his expandable leash would stretch. The dogs started the typical puppy play, jumping, licking, nipping, and then crashing when their baby energy gave out. They revived quickly and the good-natured rough housing resumed. We arranged a play date so Charlie's social circle enlarged.

He would start the morning with his next-door friend, go for his walk, and greet anything on legs, although bicycles, and skateboards were OK also. Babies in strollers were desirable, too, along with their bottles, blankets, and toys. Late afternoon was Oskar time. Did they play! The dogs chased each other around the backyard at incredible speed. Oskar's baritone described his joy. Charlie had as good a holiday as we did, with plans to return the following year.

During the pandemic, we adapted, calling/barking greetings to each other over the Covid 6-foot moat – it was easy to hear Oskar, with his bloodhound voice. And now, 11 years later, we live three doors down from the rental property of Charlie's first family vacation. Oliver is no longer with us after living a good dog life, but Charlie's group has expanded. Even though both the people and the dogs have aged, those who can join Charlie's canine community and come along every evening. As we begin our walk, people and their dogs emerge from their houses and converge in our driveway. Charlie – at this point the patriarch – checks them off the list and starts off. The big, noisy group just naturally follows.

A GOAT Named Brady Killed Our Dog

– Lisa Chayet Sahlberg –

As native Bay Staters, my husband and I grew up cheering for the New England Patriots. Many current fans may not recall or even believe that the '70s and '80s were challenging times to be a Pats fan. To be honest, it was downright depressing. We couldn't have foreseen that the New England Patriots would win even one Super Bowl title, much less six.

The year 2002 was one of firsts for us. Our first Super Bowl victory was the year we got a puppy, our first as a family. He was a 4-pound ball of energy: A brown, black, and white Rat Terrier. Now, he had a home, but he needed a name. We tossed around a few but ultimately settled on a final two: Tedy Bruschi, another favorite Patriots player, and Brady. We held a family vote, and it was unanimous; another Brady was destined to steal our hearts.

Our little puppy had some things in common with his namesake. He was fiercely loyal, intelligent, and energetic. Some differences were evident as well. Brady was incredibly agile, super-fast (clocked at 35 mph), and could vertically jump like nobody's business. Of course, these athletic traits belonged to our Brady. However, out of fairness, it must be that the other Brady could throw a football way more accurately than our puppy.

Our Brady was a loyal Pats fan. He watched every game with us and wasn't bothered by all the screaming and cheering. He loved game day for the snacks, family time, and the friends who would come over to watch. I firmly believe that Brady played an integral role in the unparalleled success of the Pats for 18 seasons. We consistently turned around losing games in the last few moments just by rubbing his left ear. He didn't ask anything in return for helping the team; he did it because he was a true fan.

Another thing our Brady had in common with Tom Brady was his youthfulness. He seemed to be impervious to the passing of time. At age 15, he still loved to run, leap over stone walls, and was the first to jump in the car for any trip. At 16, whenever Brady met a new friend out on a walk, they'd ask how old he was and marvel at his energy, not believing his age. Upon turning 17, he was still doing so well that I recall someone asking – after learning his name was Brady – if he had embraced the TB12 Diet Method. We believed that as Tom Brady was the GOAT (greatest of all time) quarterback, our Brady was the GOAT of Rat Terriers.

The Pats ended 2019 with a winning regular season, but they had to win a wild-card game to advance to the playoffs. Where was the fight and burning desire to win? Tom Brady seemed tired or maybe disinterested. Our sweet dog also started fading during this time – no more running, leaping, or eagerly examining his bowl for extra treats. He was definitely slowing down and had a few health scares but always rallied. As much as we wanted to deny it, there seemed to be a slow leak in our Brady balloon.

Our Brady's energy and joy diminished. His desire to be with us stayed, but he was declining. Minor health scares intensified, and our hearts were broken. We had to say goodbye to our amazing dog.

Could it be a mere coincidence that everything was wonderful for 18 years and once Tom Brady announced he was leaving, there was an immediate, almost palpable, decline in our Brady? OK, I know that the Pats' GOAT didn't kill the Dog GOAT and we give nothing but thanks to both for all the joy they brought us.

The Abominable Snowman and a Vanishing Act

– Lynne Abensohn –

When I was a single mom with teenagers in a new town, my daughter and son decided that an energetic American Boxer would add another dimension to our otherwise quiet suburban life. Sandy was leaving for college the following year and Ethan had two more years of high school. A new puppy would be a welcome friend and companion for Ethan to make up for being left behind.

We did our research, made some calls, and eventually found Boxer puppies that were old enough to be weaned from their mother. One spring Saturday morning, we drove to the breeder's home where Sandy and Ethan picked out a tiny pup from the litter. We were told that this petite female was the runt. She wore a pink collar and they had named her Pinky Tuscadero, after a character from "Grease."

The breeder let the kids play with all of the puppies while I signed the papers and took care of the business side of things. She then wrapped Pinky in a small soft baby blanket and handed her to Ethan. It was love at first sight. Ethan held her carefully and brought her outside to the car, opened the door, and slid across the backseat. He closed the door cautiously and held her close to his chest. He listened to her intermittent puppy snores and snorts and watched her sleep all the way home.

We had a long drive from the South Shore to Wellesley, where our Chinese friend, Angela, waited for us on our front porch. She stood under the housewarming chimes she had given us to ward off bad luck. She knew we were bringing a new family member home that afternoon, and was as excited as we were. We pulled into the driveway, jumped out of the car, and walked over to her. Then, Ethan put the little wiggly bundle in her arms.

"Her name is Pinky," Sandy announced. "Pinky Tuscadero," she added grinning with delight.

Angela looked intently at the dog, then me, then the kids.

"You should name her Ginger, she announced firmly.

"Why would you call her that?" Ethan questioned.

"Because she is precious, like ancient Chinese spice," said Angela. "She will bring zest and vitality to your life. It's a good name for this pet."

As it turned out, Angela was right. We all decided it was perfect.

Within five months, you would never guess that Ginger had been the runt of the litter. With lots of food and exercise, she was growing in every way. Her legs were becoming long and lanky and her personality was shining through. She was smart, strong, and energetic. Her sleek fawn-colored body and flashy markings were compellingly beautiful. Her face and ears were tricolored; her round droll eyes and square-shaped nose were black, as were the tips of her brown floppy ears.

Her coloration included a vertical white streak that ran from her nose up between her eyes to her forehead. But that line was not symmetrical. It veered a bit to the left, so whenever you looked at her, there was always something slightly off-kilter. Her black and white fuzzy, droopy jowls hung way below her jawline and felt softer than velvet. When she ran, those jowls flapped furiously from side to side, slapping her face silly.

Just like kids, dogs need more than food. They need love, affection, and playtime. Ginger loved to play and Ethan was, by far, her favorite playmate. When he came home from school and opened the front door, Ginger would be there waiting for him with her full body wiggle. And at the end of that wiggle was a tiny stub of a tail that spun faster than a whirligig.

"Do you want to go for a walk?" Ethan would ask her. She'd stand up on her hind legs and lick his face like an ice cream cone. She would sit alertly while he put the leash on her and then they would walk to Perrin Park where all the neighborhood dogs were allowed to run free. Later, when they got home from the park, Ethan would take her to the backyard where they would play catch.

One day Ethan gave Ginger an 8-inch stuffed Abominable Snowman Monster. This toy was a snowman-like creature with wild, woolly white hair, google eyes, a bright red mouth, jagged teeth, and sharp claws. "Grrr," Ginger growled when Ethan first showed it to her. And with that, Ginger scurried under the kitchen table.

Dogs are like siblings to kids, and Ginger was their constant companion, fun and funny, a loyal cuddle buddy Ethan affectionately teased her. Every day after school, he pulled the snowman out of the toy box and placed it on the kitchen floor. Ginger would then hesitantly walk toward it, look down at it, and start yowling. "Yowl, Yowl, Yowl." Ethan responded, "Yowl, Yowl, Yowl." Then Ginger would return the yowl. If Sandy was home, she'd get in the act, too. Then I would join in, all of us yowling together in the house! It certainly made coming home from school a special event for Ethan.

One day, Ethan accidentally left the Abominable Snowman Monster outside the back door. When no one was watching, Ginger grabbed it and headed off behind the tool shed. Ten minutes later, we went back there to see what Ginger was doing. All we could see was a deep hole, and clumps of dirt flying up in our faces as Ginger dug deeper and deeper into the mulch pile. The wild-looking snowman hung from her mouth. When she saw us standing there watching her, she dropped the toy into the pit, its final resting place. She then walked away, with her stubby tail pointing straight out. She was done with the teasing. Done with the yowling. Done, done, done.

One day, around Halloween, Ethan was away playing sports after school. Sandy was in college. I had just come back home from shopping and knew the dog had to go out. I opened the back door before unpacking the groceries. Ginger immediately ran outside and began running around the gazebo. When all of my refrigerated goods were put away, I looked out the kitchen window, again. She was still running, happy ears flapping behind her. I finally put all of the groceries away and opened the back door.

"Ginger!" I called out. It was silent. I didn't see or hear her running. "Ginger!" I yelled.

She must be around the side of the house, I thought. But no. She wasn't around the side of the house. She wasn't near the gazebo, not behind the tool shed, not at the gate. She was gone! Gone? How could that be? The fence was well over 4 and a half feet high. No holes were under it, so she hadn't dug her way out. I was in a panic. I called animal control, my friends, the neighbors, and finally the police.

"Ginger, Ginger," I called frantically at the back door and then the front door. She couldn't have escaped. My thoughts were jumbled. Route 9 is only three blocks away... So is busy Weston Road... She will most certainly be hit by a car... She could be killed... If anything happens to Ginger, I'll never forgive myself....The kids won't ever forgive me, especially Ethan.

I decided to walk to Perrin Park, where Ethan often took her. No sign. Nowhere to be found. Nothing. Nada. I walked home and sat at the kitchen table wondering what to do next. My head and heart were pounding. My body was tense. I wanted to cry.

It seemed like hours, but within minutes, my cell phone rang. "Are you the owner of a female Boxer?" a man inquired. "I found this number on her tag."

"Yes, yes! Oh! You have Ginger! Is she all right?" I yelled into the phone.

"Yes. I'm at a gas station on Route 9 near Overbrook Drive.

She's shaking a bit, but she's fine."

"Route 9?" I gasped. I was amazed Ginger wasn't hurt.

"I'll be there in less than 3 minutes."

As I approached the Shell gas station, I saw a tall young man standing outside an old blue Honda. He was holding Ginger by the collar.

I pulled into the parking lot, left the car running, and rushed toward the blue-jeaned man and Ginger.

"Thank you! Oh my God! She's never done this before." As soon as I was standing in front of her, I reached out and gave her a full-body hug. Ginger licked my fingers and wiggled her long body. I looked at him with appreciation and relief.

"How did you find her?" I asked. "I was driving down the highway and saw this beautiful dog just standing there in the middle of the road, so I came to a gradual stop, got out of my car, talked calmly to her, grabbed her by the nape of her neck, then put her in my car," he said. "I couldn't let her just stand there in the traffic. I was surprised she wasn't afraid of me."

"I'm surprised, too," I said, blinking in disbelief. "She's usually a nervous nellie around strangers."

"How do you think she escaped?" he asked.

"To tell you the truth, I have no idea. She has never jumped the fence before, and I can't imagine how she did it. It was like a vanishing act!

"Please let me give you something for saving our family pet," I pleaded.

"Nah, that won't be necessary," he said.

"But you don't understand what this means to my family and me..."

"Well, I was just on the way to my girlfriend's house, and I saw that poor nervous Boxer just standing out there."

"Are you sure I can't give you money, or a dinner out or..."

"No, no thank you. I'm good. I'm just happy I could help."

I asked him to wait a minute while I walked Ginger to the car and put her in the back seat. On the seat, I noticed the two large pumpkins I had picked up at the farm earlier in the day. I selected the larger of the two and went back to the young man.

"Here, take this to your girlfriend. You can tell her the whole story. You can tell her how you were a hero today..." He looked at me with a grin, hugged me, and took the pumpkin with both hands.

"My girlfriend will love this. Thank you so much. You've got a really nice dog there. You and your dog stay safe now. Good luck..."

"Bye. And thank you," I said with grateful tears in my eyes. "You saved a life today."

"Or maybe two," I whispered under my breath.

My Days With Wonder the Foster

– Robert Spinazzola –

Soon after volunteering at a local dog shelter, a brutal lesson came along. I realized how tough things can be for dogs in the rural South.

A young Redbone Coonhound, tall and leggy with characteristically long, floppy hound ears, was brought in so emaciated and weak she was named Wonder. It was a wonder she was still alive.

Likely turned loose by a hunter who no longer found her useful, a too-common practice here, Wonder still craved attention and would give you a slow wag of her tail when you held her head and gently stroked her ragged coat. Having been starved down to perhaps half of her proper body weight, with every single rib on prominent display and each protruding vertebrae showing the clear line of her spine, she was a sad and shocking sight.

Wonder was not a small dog, but I could nearly encircle her vanishing waist by touching my opposing thumbs and middle fingers together, something you had to see to believe. I was new to rescue but had seen enough to know this poor girl needed special care if she was to recover her strength and spirit. After arranging to take Wonder as my first-ever medical foster, I crated my other dogs in my truck's camper shell. I then carefully lifted Wonder onto the bench seat beside me and headed home. She was quiet as we rode, only occasionally lifting her head to give me a look and make sure all was well. Her survival and eventual return to good health now rested in my hands. Was I up to the challenge? I shook off any nagging doubts as the miles went by and resolved to give this sweet girl the best care I possibly could – I only hoped it would be enough.

I knew little about hounds and even less about how to help a dog recover from this type of neglect. I consulted with the shelter's primary vet, did much online research, and developed a plan for Wonder. It turns out that in severe cases of malnutrition, dogs can have a complete loss of appetite, with their systems on the verge of total shutdown. So it was with Wonder. Other than a quick sniff, she showed no interest when offered small meals of white rice sprinkled with bits of chicken meat and broth.

I learned that dogs in Wonder's condition should avoid large meals in favor of numerous small and balanced meals to jump-start their digestion and avoid overwhelming their system. Too much protein or fat could also cause problems, particularly with the kidneys, leading to complications and even death. Wonder and I were walking a tightrope with no safety net, a scary proposition.

The first day went by with no success, then the next. Wonder was increasingly listless. I was distraught and frustrated. The battle appeared to be over before it had begun. I started giving her enticing chicken skin and hamburger. The additions were a risk but one we needed to take, and fast. The third morning, I put breakfast down and watched carefully as Wonder gave the bowl a sniff, then a tentative nibble, then another. To my enormous relief, this walking skeleton of a dog, so desperately in need of nutrition, was finally eating. While she didn't finish it all, Wonder had taken a huge step in the right direction.

Over the next few days, I fine-tuned her meals, and gradually, Wonder's appetite began to return. After a week as my foster's personal chef, we had made great strides. She was now eating four small but growing meals daily, finishing every morsel, and showing no signs of systemic issues. While I knew Wonder was still in a delicate state, I allowed myself a growing optimism. A successful recovery now seemed within reach, and that possibility felt great.

As days turned into weeks and Wonder's recovery kicked into high gear, she began enjoying more time outside in the fenced yard with the other dogs, even showing enough zip to engage in short bouts of closely supervised play. I began to walk her on the wooded paths behind the house and to my surprise, Wonder, unlike many hounds, had excellent leash manners. Our jaunts became a pleasure and a bonding experience for us both. While Wonder got along well with all my dogs, it was clear that Zellie, my athletic female and likely agility dog in some past life, was her favorite. Soon, Zellie, the best of my dogs on leash, began joining Wonder and me on these walks, wandering through the woods, soaking in the quiet, the cool shade, and the tantalizing scents – an absolute pleasure for us all.

After three months, Wonder had made impressive progress. She still had a bit of weight to gain, but she had filled out, the shine had returned to her coat, and she had the energy befitting a sporting dog. The most challenging part of Wonder's recovery was over, so the search for an organization that could help her find a forever home began. Over time, my foster and I had grown quite close. Wonder had become what we in rescue call a "Velcro" dog. She followed me everywhere, lapped up every bit of attention she could get, and never strayed far. I found that when Wonder and I walked alone, I no longer needed a leash as she stayed right by my side, an unusual trait for any dog, much less a nose-driven hound. She had come a long way, and the bittersweet moment of writing the next chapter of her remarkable story was now at hand.

Having five dogs, taking on a sixth seemed beyond what I could manage, so one of the shelter's rescue partners in Pennsylvania agreed to help. Wonder was scheduled to head to Pennsylvania within the month, but as my days with her counted down, I struggled with doubts about the decision to let her go. She had been through so much and yet was still a happy, affectionate girl, but my dogs deserved more time with me. Could I give them all the time, attention, and love they deserved? These are the questions those in rescue face.

I had the chance to speak with Linda in Pennsylvania, whose family was set to take Wonder, and our talk brought me much comfort. Linda had a great situation with a large, fenced yard, another friendly dog about Wonder's size, lots of dog experience, and, most importantly, a true and compassionate heart. With my mind eased, it was settled: Wonder would travel North.

The transport was scheduled to leave early on a Saturday morning. In the days leading up to her departure, I spent most of my available time exclusively with Wonder, a fact not lost on my other dogs. Friday we all traveled up to my rescue friend's 60-acre horse property, where the dogs and I often stayed during shelter visits. That last evening, in the day's dwindling light, I took Wonder for one final walk around the paths my dogs and I had come to know so well. This last walk, this last special moment together, was just for Wonder. As we walked, many conflicting emotions bubbled up in me – gratitude for the support and guidance received while fighting for this dog, a deep sadness that I would no longer be the one looking after her, but most of all, a heartfelt appreciation of the company, love, and education Wonder had given me.

As we approached the house, Wonder did something that caught me completely off guard. I saw her ears rise and her nose sniff the air, and then, in an instant, she was off, bounding across a pasture in the now rapidly failing light before disappearing into the woods beyond, baying her best hound bay all the while. I followed her, calling her name over and over to no avail. I could hear her crashing through the brush, but I had no idea what had caught her attention. Why, after months of coming to me every time I called, was she now ignoring my increasingly panicked pleas? After 10 minutes or so of trying to keep up with her and calling her a hundred times with no success, it suddenly occurred to me that here, just hours from sending her on to a better life, I might lose her forever. This foreboding thought sent chills down my spine, but suddenly, inspiration struck: I had to go get Zellie, Wonder's best buddy, to lead her out of those dark woods and back to safety.

I ran as fast as possible and grabbed a leash and flashlight. I yelled for Zellie, my faithful girl, to follow me outside and back to the edge of the woods. I could still hear Wonder's occasional bay, fainter and further away but still within earshot, which was a ray of hope. I sent Zellie into the woods with the instructions to "go get Wonder" and followed as best I could by the meager beam of the flashlight, adrenaline-fueled desperation pushing me on. Five minutes passed, then 10.

Sounds of the dogs came and went, and my continued calls became less frequent. It couldn't end like this. I couldn't lose Wonder now. I knew Zellie would find her way out of those woods as she knew every inch of this property, having wandered it so often in the years since coming to me, but would Wonder follow? The question hung heavily on me as I returned to the pasture and waited by the edge of the woods.

Finally, after what seemed an eternity, I heard the unmistakable noise of a dog approaching. Out of the woods popped Zellie, her black outline hard to see in the now nearly complete darkness as the flashlight's battery ran low. Seconds later, Wonder followed, with both dogs bounding up to greet me after their chaotic nighttime adventure. I quickly clipped the leash to Wonder's collar to avoid additional shenanigans and let out a massive sigh of relief. The tension, worry, and resolve all drained from me at once, leaving me exhausted and limp after a chaotic and harrowing 30 minutes. With the situation now under control, I took a moment to stand quietly, loving on both dogs while searching for my lost composure, hoping I hadn't left it forever somewhere out in those woods. Finally gathering myself, I led the dogs back to the safe harbor of the house where we might rest and recover, myself most of all.

With the dogs settled in for the night, I finally crawled into bed. Just before nodding off, the meaning of Wonder's last-minute romp came to me – it was a sign that she had made it back from the brink, both physically and emotionally, to find her true, scent-driven hound spirit once again. My quest to help her was successful and complete. With that pleasant thought, I floated off to a restful sleep.

Wonder made the morning transport, and her foster Linda fell totally in love, soon making Wonder her very own, a happy ending to a nearly disastrous story. Wonder went on to live into a ripe old age, and over the years Linda and I stayed in touch, with each update leaving me slightly wistful.

This hound girl taught me many things, but the most important was the truth about foster dogs: In time, they may leave your care, leave your home, and leave your life, but they will never, ever leave your heart.

About the Authors

LYNNE MATHEWS ABENSOHN:

THE ABOMINABLE SNOWMAN AND A VANISHING ACT

Lynne grew up in the smallest city in the smallest state of the Union but is a lifelong traveler. For the past 13 years, she has taught business, marketing, and ESL at Showa Boston, a branch of Showa Women's University, Tokyo. Her avocations include cooking, singing, and organic gardening. She has two adult children and lives in Newton, Mass.

NANCY BRIGHAM:

WE CALLED HER BRIGID FOR THE SAINT

Nancy has never owned a dog, but she is not above foisting a puppy on a friend, thus starting a love affair between man and dog that extended over many years. Nancy lives in Lexington, Mass., where she keeps busy writing picture books about the adventures of Macaroon Mouse, which are available on amazon.com.

LEN CHARNEY:

MOLLY'S LAIR

Len lives in Rowley, Mass., with his wife, Steffi, and their 2-year-old Goldendoodle, Henry. Most days are spent cooking up a storm, tinkering in the shop, enjoying scenic North Shore bike rides, writing stories about his past, and imagining the future through the eyes of his grandson, Cooper, age 1.

JON CLAFLIN:

MIDNIGHT RESCUE

Jon made the journey from standup comedian to comedy writer back in the '90s. He has published stories in various places, including his previous publication, All True News. Jon now enjoys writing true short stories and is working on two books, dividing his time between Massachusetts and Maine. A heart transplant recipient, Jon is grateful for every day.

ANDREA CLEGHORN:

IT STARTED WITH MR. PERKINS

A recovering journalist – now coaching writers and running memoir classes – Andrea got her first legit job out of journalism school at Teen Magazine. She has worked for weekly papers, tabloids, and magazines, as well as has written a few books, including The Whipple Brunch and Rosie's Place. She's the creator of "Dispatches From Ireland," on video and print.

KATE COTTER:

WAITING FOR SCOUT

Kate is the author of many full journals and essays that have been safely tucked away in boxes or computers. She is ecstatic that one of them is being released into the wild! She lives in Newburyport, Mass., with her family, Kona the wonder dog, and a 5-pound bunny who scares Kona daily, but that's another story.

DEBORAH D'AVOLIO, Ph.D.:
POOLSIDE CODE BLUE
Deborah recently retired from her faculty role with a specialty in gerontological research and practice. Her hobbies are traveling, writing, reading, and knitting. Deborah enjoys spending time with family, friends, and her dog, Kylee, and cat, Boo Boo.

SUSAN ELLIS:
OUR MOUNTAIN GIRL AWAITS
Susan Ellis is a writer, teacher, and dog lover with a passion for the outdoors. Recently retired from an interesting and exciting career in corporate communications and training, she now lives in Phippsburg, Maine. Susan enjoys learning fiddle, studying Mandarin, gardening, traveling, writing, and reading.

DONAL FITZGERALD:
A DOG'S VIEW
Donal Fitzgerald from Cork lives in scenic Kenmare with his husband Nick from England and their two little dogs, a Miniature Schnauzer and a Yorkie – an international family. Retired from a lifetime in healthcare, Donal determined his next care is living life to the full, traveling, gardening, writing, reading, and nurturing his creativity. It's a new chapter full of promise.

BRENDA FRASER:

WHAT'S FOR DINNER?

Brenda Fraser is a life-long adopter of strays. From dogs and cats to children and friends, if you don't have a place to call home, she will take you in and make one for you. A lifelong resident of Massachusetts, Brenda works in high tech to support her crafting, reading, and writing passions.

JUNE HUNTER:

NO PERMANENT NAME

June Hunter lives and writes in Sneem, County Kerry, Ireland. Her work has been featured in various publications, including Flash Fiction Magazine, Reflex Fiction, Potato Soup Journal, Blue Nib, Strands Publishers, and Bloom. She facilitates the Sneem Writers' Group and participates in Clann na Farraige Writers' Group, Kenmare. June also takes part in "Deadlines for Writers" online writing challenges.

ANN HERLIHY JARONCYK:

PROMISES KEPT AND BROKEN

Ann's love of dogs began when she read about Dick and Jane and their dog, Spot. Ann, now retired and without a furry friend, often cares for various pets whose owners travel. This new venture is a perfect fit.

GENE KALB:

ARE DOGS JUST STUDYING US?

Part-time writer, full-time entrepreneur. Gene grew up a cat person, at one point with a business importing catnip (no kidding). Gene got his first dog at 46, and now he and his wife have Dodge, a prominent

Black Lab mix rescue. "Dogs have filled a social hole in our lives – these fellow dog walkers are a blessing!

DONNA KEEFE:
MY DOG DANCED
Donna is a designer, artist, author, and advocate for recycling and public art who recognizes how art and design can positively impact our daily lives. Living near the ocean, she draws inspiration from its restorative powers to fuel her creative pursuits.

JOSEPH LAFO:
A LOVING TRIBUTE TO RASCAL
Joseph has been a practicing architect for 50 years and began personal writing in earnest in 2008 when he became disciplined to take advantage of the pleasure he derives from it. Since then, he has written about 1,000 essays of varying lengths, documenting life events and memories for his sons and grandchildren.

KATHLEEN MACKIN, Ph.D.:
MAGGIE, UNDAUNTED
Kathie is an educational psychologist who, throughout her career, worked as a teacher, educational researcher, and program evaluator. She always had a dog at her feet or a cat sleepily sprawled across her desk, with the background click-clack sound of typing. Now pet-free in Stratham, N.H., she is on the lookout for her next loving writing companion.

REBECCA MAYER:

DAD SAID NO DOGS

As a psychologist, Rebecca wrote patient reports and grants. In retirement, she experiments with autobiographical writing. After Chippy, Rebecca had two Border Collies and now has a Chiweenie. Eventually, she fulfilled her dream of having horses, the first one a thoroughbred. She and her husband imported and bred Norwegian fjord horses, 22 at one point!

HELEN MORSE:

ADORABLE PSYCHOPATH

Helen is a lifelong photographer and visual artist who recently published a memoir called The Difficult Girl. She is passionate about self-expression in all its forms and has always been an animal lover. Once, she even shared her home with a foundling snapping turtle named Frederico. These days, Helen lives on Plum Island, Mass.

CAROLE NOVECK:

CHARLIE, THE COMMUNITY-BUILDING COCKALIER

Carole has enjoyed all her seven dogs through the years, beginning with an adopted Beagle up to Charlie, her current Spaniel mix. Carole is a retired teacher, formerly in a university-based special education program, and now tutors English as a Second Language. "Dogs and family are the constants of my life," she says.

BEN PETERSON:

ANOTHER ROUND OF NELLIE

Ben directs the Architectural Futures Group at the Boston Society for Architecture. Originally from Boston's South Shore and now a Cambridge resident, he is a designer, educator, and willing tag-along for adventures with his Australian Shepherd, Nellie. This essay is Ben's first.

JEN PILIERO:
OTIS, THE CARING CANINE
Jen, human companion to faithful, adventurous, and mischievous Pluto, lives in Bedford, Mass., with her partner Susan and son Sam. Jen's first canine was Otis, a delightful, goofy Goldendoodle who shared his sweet self with the family and as a visiting therapy dog. Pluto has followed in Otis's paw steps and is now a proud member of Caring Canines.

DONNA RICCI:
THE BEAGLE RESCUER
Donna works to weave her passions as a psychologist, USA Archery Coach, and musician into her essays to create harmony and resonance. While she does not currently live with any dogs, she stays open to the possibility that any day, they might grace her with their presence.

BRENDA RIDDELL:
LOST AND FOUND
Brenda is a graphic designer, educator, and entrepreneur. She is the owner and creative director at Graphic Details, Inc., a print and web design studio in Portsmouth, N.H. Brenda is passionate about animal welfare. She has volunteered with several animal rescues and is the creator of **artfortheunderdog.com** and **straightoffthestreets.com**, websites aimed at raising awareness of animal homelessness and neglect.

LISA CHAYET SAHLBERG:
A GOAT NAMED BRADY KILLED MY DOG
Lisa lived in Massachusetts before her recent move to Maine. Living on a beautiful lake and spending as much time outdoors as possible, she has endless opportunities to photograph birds, flowers, and little bits and pieces of nature. She also enjoys baking, reading, and writing.

ROBERT SPINAZZOLA:
MY TIME WITH WONDER THE FOSTER
Bob has been involved at the Mary Ann Morris Animal Society, aka MAMAS Shelter, in rural S.C. since 2007. He helped the shelter become no-kill and sent more than 13,000 dogs off to better lives. Bob hopes you'll consider adopting from or volunteering for your local shelter, since many are struggling. He is pleased to share the story of one special southern dog here.

JENNY STEWART:
MY HEART AND THE QUIET ONES
Jenny Stewart insisted on being called Scottie for a few years as a kid while she pretended to be a dog of that breed. She likes the woods, making cookies, playing games, and listening to stories. Her dogs have always had human names.

ANDREA STOEHR:
KEALIE: A BLACK DOG RESCUED
Andrea lives in Danby, Vt., with her husband Ed, her dog, Kealie, her cat, Sylvie, and a variety of very free-range chickens. Andrea is a painter and illustrator as well as a hostess to an AirBnB with majestic mountain views in every direction.

MARIANA STONE:
EMOTIONAL SUPPORT DOG
Mariana lives in Boston with her husband, daughter, and loyal pup. In her free time, she enjoys gardening, reading, and cooking. Izzy will always be Mariana's first baby and the best dog a girl could want.

ROBERT UDULUTCH:
THE FATE OF SPOT AND SMUDGE
Just a Wisconsin boy whose first job was pumping poo out of RVs while reading everything he could get his smelly hands on. Bob now travels a lot and pens his experiences with rescued littermate pups in the Spot and Smudge series and the One Paw in the Grave collection.

STACEY NEWMAN WELDON:
DOG IS OUR CO-PILOT
Stacey Newman Weldon ignited her love for writing a decade ago. Leaving behind her high-flying career in media sales, she's now fetching a living as a freelance writer, covering various topics. Brady's spirit as her faithful co-pilot inspired her to pen his story.

EMELINE LO-PILIERO (**IN KIDS' CORNER**):
MY HERO, THE AMAZING MAISIE
Emeline has been a fan of Goldendoodles since she was 7 and spent a summer with relatives in Bedford, meeting Doodles Maisie and Pluto. In school that following year, she was asked to write about her hero, "so naturally it was about Maisie." Now Emeline's 12 and has her very own dog, Lily – a Goldendoodle, of course!

COOPER OGDEN (**IN KIDS' CORNER**):
A DOG: THE BEST PET TO GET!
Cooper, 9, lives in Ipswich, Mass. His interests include Nintendo, Rubik's Cube challenges, catching sea creatures, and soccer. His team just won the 4x4 Challenge at Gillette Stadium! His favorite types of books involve fighter jets and dragons. Cooper enjoys playing with his two brothers and his Puerto Rican rescue dogs, Puchi and Cesar.

LAURA WALS (**IN KIDS' CORNER**):
WE LOVE OUR BUCKETHEAD
Laura, 12, lives with her parents and dog Kaya in the Netherlands. In addition to taking care of Kaya, Laura loves being creative and enjoys drawing, making jewelry for both humans and dolls and crocheting colorful bandanas for her four-legged friends.

Acknowledgments

In late 2022, we in New England were facing the familiar prospect of a cold, desolate winter. Covid was coming back and it felt as if bad news was also on the rise, manmade and all-natural, here and in far-away places. Focusing on a feel-good project seemed like a great idea; if we could raise some money for a worthy cause, all the better.

In the spirit of "let's have a show!" a couple of us came up with the idea of putting together an anthology of true, never-before-published stories about our dogs, always a favorite topic of conversation.

Dogs make us happy. They inspire us to be better by example; they're funny, clever, loyal, and are always delighted to see us. They show us what it's like to live in the day. They don't care if they are being ridiculous. They catch us when we fall – OK, sometimes *cause* us to fall – then lick our faces when we are down, literally or figuratively.

We needed to find some help, so we got together an editorial committee of five of us friends. We are Elizabeth Banks, a journalist who's worked at newspapers in the Boston area. Kevin Fahey, Professor Emeritus at Salem State University, is now focusing on writing memoirs and short stories. Nancy Brigham recently retired from a career in education research and program evaluation; she currently writes books for children and young adults. Len Charney is Dean Emeritus, at Boston Architectural College, and is a writer. And I, as chair, am the fifth member. I coach nonfiction writers in workshops and individually.

After the committee was set, we all contacted friends, and friends of friends, who had a story to tell and were interested in doing an essay in the range of 1000 words. Many of the participants from my memoir classes at Newburyport Adult and Community Education jumped in to answer the call and have stories on these pages. To represent the next generation of writers, Emeline Lo-Piliero, Cooper Ogden, and Laura Wals, have written delightful stories for the Kids' Corner, pages 51-56.

Nancy Daugherty, our book designer, pulled everything together. She has been creative, dedicated, and unflappable.

Be sure to check out Len Charney's story, "Molly's Lair" on page 45. It tells how college classmates Len and Kevin – from this committee – adopted Molly, a Lab/German Shepherd. Back then she was a lively pup frolicking on the dog-friendly Cornell campus who ended up getting herself into trouble of the age-old variety. Molly is pictured years later on the front of this book, relaxing in the sun with Len's mom Etta Rose. At this point, both were golden-agers, companions taking care of each other.

All proceeds from Dog Tales go to Caring Canines, a Boston area visiting dog therapy organization. Volunteers take their trained pets to nursing homes and treatment centers. Read one first-hand account on page 119, "Otis, the Therapy Dog." Lately, there have been more requests than ever to enlist their special brand of canine comfort. Despite the all-volunteer running of the program, there are costs. For information about this nonprofit, go to **www.caringcanines.org**.

I thank everybody who worked on Dog Tales, a labor of love in every case.

Andrea Cleghorn, chair
Dog Lovers Committee: Elizabeth Banks, Nancy Brigham, Len Charney, and Kevin Fahey

December 2023

Made in United States
Troutdale, OR
12/21/2023

16318639R00098